INTRODUCTION TO E

REVISION GUID

C000060679

EU Law Book by Dr Çınar is different than other textbooks in the market, as it is designed to make sense of a complex area of law in a simple yet comprehensive way. The book contains materials relating to EU law with all the notable cases and materials collected in one place. It is written in plain language in the form of question and answers. At the end of each chapter, there is a case study which helps to put theory into practice. EU Law is accessible, readable and user- friendly. I would recommend it without hesitation to legal scholars and practitioners.

Dr Aysem Diker Vanberg, Senior Lecturer, University of Greenwich

This clear and concise book provides a practical overview of EU law and will be an excellent study aid for law students. It explains the key topics of EU law in an accessible and engaging manner through a Q&A model and case studies that demonstrate how the law is applied.

Dr Johanna Hoekstra, Lecturer, University of Essex

The is an accessible, easy to read and very useful book covering all the essential areas of EU law making them easily understood.

Dr Marios Costa, Senior Lecturer, City Law School, University of London

INTRODUCTION TO EU LAW

REVISION GUIDE

DR ÖZGÜR HEVAL ÇINAR

TRANSNATIONAL PRESS LONDON

2021

Law Series: 1

INTRODUCTION TO EU LAW - REVISION GUIDE

By Dr Özgür Heval Çınar

Copyright © 2021 Transnational Press London

First published in 2021 by TRANSNATIONAL PRESS LONDON in the United Kingdom, 12 Ridgeway Gardens, London, N6 5XR, UK.

www.tplondon.com

Transnational Press London® and the logo and its affiliated brands are registered trademarks.

Requests for permission to reproduce material from this work should be sent to: admin@tplondon.com

Paperback

ISBN: 978-1-80135-029-7

Digital

ISBN: 978-1-912997-93-0

Cover Design: Nihal Yazgan

www.tplondon.com

CONTENTS

ABBREVIATIONS

CEE: Charges having an equivalent effect to a customs duty

CJEU: Court of Justice of the European Union

CMLR: Common Market Law Reports

EC: European Community

ECR: European Court Reports

ECSC: European Coal and Steel Community

EEC: European Economic Community

EU: European Union

MEQR: Measures having equivalent effect to a quantitative restriction

QR: Quantitative Restrictions

SQE: Solicitors Qualifying Examination

TEU: Treaty on European Union

TFEU: Treaty on the Functioning of the European Union

UK: United Kingdom

ABOUT THE AUTHOR

Dr Özgür Heval Çınar is a lawyer. Presently, he is an associate professor at the University of Greenwich, School of Law and Criminology. He completed his PhD at the School of Law, University of Essex. Previously, he was a post-doc fellow at the University of Oxford between 2012-2016.

FOREWORD

It is a well-known fact that there was frequent bloody conflict in Europe for hundreds of years. These wars caused widespread death and destruction. As a result of these devastating losses, European leaders and thinkers such as Robert Schuman (French Foreign Minister) and Jean Monnet (the first Secretary General of the League of Nations) realised that the only way to achieve a sustainable peace was to combine the political and economic resources of countries. Consequently, in 1951 the European Coal and Steel Community (ECSC) was founded, involving Belgium, the Federal Republic of Germany (West Germany), Luxembourg, France, Italy and the Netherlands. This association was the first step to establishing the European Union (EU). Hence, in 1957 it was decided to found an economic community based on the free movement of labour, goods and services. This eventually developed into the present EU, which has 27 members. Apart from these countries, there are 5 countries that have candidate member status.

The relationship of the United Kingdom (UK) to the EU has from the outset been the subject of numerous academic and non-academic studies. At the referendum of June 2016, the decision to leave the EU was taken and after a long process the UK officially left the EU on 31 January 2020. Moreover, the Trade and Cooperation Agreement was signed by the EU and the UK on 30 December 2020. It is applicable since 1 January 2021. However, existing relations with the EU are still ambiguous at the time these lines were written.

In this process, the Solicitors Regulation Authority and Bar Standards Board still require this course to be taught in faculties of law at UK universities. In addition, certainly, in other EU member states and candidate member states EU law is part of the curriculum in legal education.

The real reason for the emergence of this book is that other publications do not explain such a complex issue in plain language, which makes it very difficult for those taking an interest, in particular law students. Moreover, experience of teaching this course for many years and particularly knowing the fields in which students experience difficulties, made me aware of the need for such a work. This book does not repeat material that is available in many textbooks that are in print. Rather, it endeavours to present every topic in plain language and concludes every chapter with a fictitious explanatory sample case. In other words, it is an introduction to the subject of EU Law, the objective of which is

5

to explain the topic both theoretically and in its application dimension. Additionally, this book will assist students in preparing for courseworks/examinations. At the end of the book, there is also a test that summarizes all the subjects contained in the book, which is appropriate to the first stage SQE (Solicitors Qualifying Examination) examination model that will be introduced on 1 September 2021. I hope this book will help all those who have an interest in this subject.

I would also like to express my gratitude to all those at Transnational Press London who provided their full support, and to Prof İbrahim Sirkeci, Mr Andrew Penny, Ms Hülya Ak and to others who contributed that I am unable to name individually here.

Dr Özgür Heval Çınar

CHAPTER I

INTRODUCTION: HISTORY, SOURCES AND INSTITUTIONS

Learning Outcomes:

In this chapter, you should be able to understand:

- ✓ the history of the European Union (EU);
- ✓ the different acts of the EU and its sources of law;
- ✓ the EU's institutions and their functions.

Questions and Answers:

1. **Why do you still need to study the EU Law despite the fact the UK withdrew its membership from the EU?**

   The Solicitors Regulation Authority and Bar Standards Board require there to be an EU Law Module. Furthermore, it is quite possible that the process of disengaging EU law from the United Kingdom (UK) law will be a protracted one. In addition, EU law will probably still have a significance in post-Brexit relations with the EU.

2. **What is the brief history of the EU?**

   1951: European Coal and Steel Community (ECSC) Treaty (Treaty of Paris). This treaty's aim was to establish a common market for coal and steel. It came into force in 1952. The original members were: Belgium; France; Italy; Luxembourg; the Netherlands and West Germany.

   1957: The Treaties of Rome. This treaty consisted of European Economic Community (EEC) Treaty and Euratom (the European Atomic Energy Community) Treaty. They were signed by the same above-mentioned members. Both treaties came into force in 1958.

   1973: United Kingdom, Ireland and Denmark joined.

   1981: Greece joined.

   1986: Spain and Portugal joined.

1986: Single European Act was signed to provide for the completion of a single internal market within the EEC.

1992: Treaty on European Union (Maastricht Treaty) was signed. It came into force in 1993. It created 'European Union' based on three fundamental pillars:

✓ Pillar I was constituted by the European Community (EC), Euratorm and originally, ECSC.
✓ Pillar II provided a framework for inter-governmental cooperation between Member States on foreign and security policy.
✓ Pillar III provided a framework for inter-governmental cooperation between Member States in specified areas concerning justice and home affairs.

In addition, this Treaty established Euro currency and European Central Bank (UK opted out Euro currency). It also contained a 'Protocol on Social Policy' (known Social Chapter) dealing with worker's rights and other social issues (UK also opted out).

1995: Austria, Finland and Sweden joined.

1997: 'Treaty of Amsterdam' was signed. The purpose of this Treaty was to enhance decision-making procedures and to make the existing treaty structure more coherent. It renumbered of the EC Treaty and Treaty on European Union (TEU).

2001: 'Treaty of Nice' was signed. It came into force in 2003. This treaty paved the way for the EU to admit a large number of new members.

2004: Cyprus, Czech Republic, Estonia, Hungary, Lithuania, Latvia, Malta, Poland, Slovakia and Slovenia joined.

2004: 'The Constitutional Treaty' was signed to provide a single constitutional framework for the EU.

2005: 'The Constitutional Treaty' rejected in popular referenda held in France and the Netherlands. It has been abandoned.

2007: Bulgaria and Romania joined.

2007: 'Treaty of Lisbon' signed. It came into force in 2009. EC Treaty renamed as 'The Treaty on the Functioning of the European Union'. It abolished three pillar structure which was created by Maastricht Treaty. In addition, amendments made to this treaty and to the Treaty on European Union.

2013: Croatia joined.

2020: UK left. The EU-UK Trade and Cooperation Agreement was signed.

2021: The Trade and Cooperation Agreement is applicable from 1 January 2021 onwards.

3. **What are the legal sources of the EU Law?**

   Primary: Treaties

   Secondary: Regulations; Directives and Decisions

   Case Law: Judgments of the EU Courts

   Soft-Law: Recommendations; Opinions and others

4. **What is a Treaty?**

   Treaty is a primary legal source in EU Law. It consists of Treaty on the Functioning of the European Union (TFEU) and Treaty on European Union (TEU). They are legally binding on member states.

5. **What is a Regulation?**

   According to Article 288 of the TFEU, regulation is a secondary legal source in EU Law. Regulations are enforceable in all Member States, coming into effect immediately without the need for any measures by these states. They are also binding on member states.

6. **What is a Directive?**

   Directives are a secondary binding legal source in EU Law. According to Article 288 of the TFEU, directives are addressed to Member States which have to implement them. Member states have the obligation to implement directives within the stated deadline in the directive. In the event the directive has no deadline, then they must be introduced within 20 days of the publication of the directive (Article 297 of the TFEU).

7. **What is a Decision?**

   According to Article 288 of the TFEU, decision is a secondary legal source in EU Law. A decision shall be binding in its entirety. A decision addressed to particular recipients shall only be binding on them.

8. What is a Case-law?

The judgments of the EU Courts: The Court of Justice of the European Union (CJEU) and the European Court of Auditors. Their judgments have binding force.

9. What is a Soft-Law?

Recommendations and opinions. According to Article 288 of the TFEU, they are not legal binding. Other forms of soft-law are such as: Communications, Declarations, Notices, Programmers and Resolutions.

10. What are the institutions of the European Union and their functions?

Council of the European Union: Composed by ministers from the Member States. Its functions are as follows: to represent the Member States' governments; to make legislations with the European Parliament; to make and coordinate policies; to sign international treaties; to scrutiny and approval of the budget with the European Parliament; to develop the EU's common foreign and security policy.[1]

Court of Justice of the European Union: Its functions are as follows: to interpret and enforce the EU law; to determine the validity of acts and legislation of the EU; to make rulings on preliminary references from national courts.[2]

European Central Bank: Its functions are as follows: to be responsible for conducting the monetary policy of these Member States; to comprise Member States which have the Euro as their currency; to maintain price stability in the EU; to co-operate with the central banks of all Member States.[3]

European Commission: Composed by one commissioner from each Member States; President of the Commission; High Representative of the Union for Foreign Affairs and Security Policy. Its functions are as follows: to initiate legislations; to administer policies and programmes; to draft the annual EU budget; to manage the budget and allocating funding; to enforce

---

[1] For further information on the Council of the European Union, see the following link: https://europa.eu/european-union/about-eu/institutions-bodies/council-eu_en

[2] For further information on the Court of Justice of the European Union, see the following link: https://europa.eu/european-union/about-eu/institutions-bodies/court-justice_en

[3] For further information on the European Central Bank, see the following link: https://europa.eu/european-union/about-eu/institutions-bodies/european-central-bank_en

EU Law; to negotiate for international treaties; to represent the EU on certain international bodies.[4]

European Council: Composited by Heads of State or Government of the Member States; President of the European Council and President of the European Commission. Its functions are as follows: to provide the necessary impetus for EU's development; to define the general political directions and priorities thereof; to deal with complex and politically sensitive issues.[5]

European Court of Auditors: Its function is as follows: to audit the revenue and expenditure of the EU.[6]

European Parliament: Composited by 766 members (MEPs) elected by the citizens of the Member States for five-year terms. Its functions are as follows: to make law; to scrutiny and approval of the EU budget; to supervise other institutions such as European Commission; to debate issues related to the EU.[7]

11. What are the key documents related to EU-UK relations?

European Communities Act 1972: The main purpose of this Act was to bring the UK into the Europe Union (previously known as 'European Economic Community'). UK Courts must follow the decisions of the European Court of Justice (Section 2 and 3).

European Union Act 2011: The main purpose of this Act was to introduce a referendum to be held on amendments of TEU or TFEU (Section 2).

European Union (Withdrawal) (No. 1) Act 2018: The main purpose of this Act was to give power to the Government to negotiate with EU to withdraw the UK's membership. In addition, Section 1 states that "The European Communities Act 1972 is repealed on exit day." Section 13 also states that "…the negotiated withdrawal agreement and the framework for the future relationship have been approved by a resolution of the House of Commons on a motion moved by a Minister of the Crown…"

---

[4] For further information on the European Commission, see the following link: https://europa.eu/european-union/about-eu/institutions-bodies/european-commission_en

[5] For further information on the European Council, see the following link: https://europa.eu/european-union/about-eu/institutions-bodies/european-council_en

[6] For further information on the European Court of Auditors, see the following link: https://europa.eu/european-union/about-eu/institutions-bodies/european-court-auditors_en

[7] For further information on the European Parliament, see the following link: https://europa.eu/european-union/about-eu/institutions-bodies/european-parliament_en

European Union (Withdrawal) (No. 2) Act 2019: The main purpose of this Act was to make further provision in connection with the period for negotiations for withdrawing from the EU (Sections 1-5).

European Union (Withdrawal) Act 2020: The main purpose of this Act to implement, and make other provision in connection with, the agreement between the UK and the EU under Article 50(2) of the TEU which sets out the arrangements for the UK's withdrawal from the EU. There are several key points as follows

- ✓ The European Communities Act 1972, as it has effect in national law or the law of a relevant territory immediately before exit day [31 January 2020 at 23.00], continues to have effect in national law or the law of the relevant territory on and after exit day so far as provided by subsections (3) to (5) (Section 1A(2)). It should be note that this Act will be effective in national law until 31 December 2020 because of implementation period (Part 1).
- ✓ The Act deals with rights in relation to entry and residence of Union Citizens as well as with financial settlement between the UK and the EU (Part 2, 3 and 4).
- ✓ This Act also underlines that " ...the Parliament of the United Kingdom is sovereign." (Section 38, Part 5).

The EU-UK Trade and Cooperation Agreement 2020: "[It] concluded between the EU and the UK sets out preferential arrangements in areas such as trade in goods and in services, digital trade, intellectual property, public procurement, aviation and road transport, energy, fisheries, social security coordination, law enforcement and judicial cooperation in criminal matters, thematic cooperation and participation in Union programmes. It is underpinned by provisions ensuring a level playing field and respect for fundamental rights."[8]

Important Treaty Articles to be Explored:

Article 2 Treaty on European Union (TEU)

Article 3 TEU

Article 5 TEU

Article 3 Treaty on the Functioning of the European Union (TFEU)

---

[8] For further information on the EU-UK Trade and Cooperation Agreement, see the following link: https://ec.europa.eu/info/relations-united-kingdom/eu-uk-trade-and-cooperation-agreement_en

Article 4 TFEU

Article 6 TFEU

Article 288 TFEU

CHAPTER II

ENFORCEMENT IN NATIONAL COURTS: SUPREMACY AND DIRECT EFFECT

Learning Outcomes:

In this chapter, you should be able to understand:

✓ the supremacy of EU law;
✓ direct effect as a method for enforcing EU law in national courts;
✓ the difference between direct effect and direct applicability;
✓ the significance of the landmark decision of the Court of Justice in Van Gend en Loos;
✓ the requirements for the provisions of EU Treaties, Regulations and Directives to have direct effect.

Questions and Answers:

1. **Define supremacy of EU law. Which case originally established it?**

   The principle of supremacy of EU law was established in the case of Costa. The applicant, Mr Costa, was a shareholder in an electrical company of Edison Volta. But the Italian Republic nationalized the production and distribution of electric energy. It also created an organisation, the Ente Nazionale Energia Elettrica (or ENEL) (National Electricity Board). All assets of the electricity undertakings were transferred to this organisation. Mr Costa refused to pay his electric bill because he claimed that the Italian nationalisation legislation was contrary to Community law (pp. 588-589).

   The CJEU stated that "the law stemming from the Treaty... could not... be overridden by domestic legal provisions, however framed" (p. 594).

   In other words, if there is any conflict between EU and national law, EU law takes precedence over national law.

2. **Define direct effect. How does it differ from direct applicability?**

   Direct effect is a facet of EU Law that grants immediate rights without Member States having to legislate. People granted these rights can claim them within the domestic systems of Member States.

Article 288 of the TFEU defines direct applicability, stating that treaties or regulations automatically become part of the national law of Member States, whereas national authorities may choose how to implement directives.

3. **Which case originally established direct effect?**

The principle of direct effect originated in the case of ***Van Gend en Loos***. In this case, a Dutch company, Van Gend en Loos as claimant, was made to pay a higher tariff when importing chemicals from West Germany to the Netherlands by Dutch customs. The company appealed against this, saying it contravened Article 12 of the EEC Treaty, which banned import duties between Member States. The Dutch authorities, the defendants, argued that since the company was not a natural person but a legal person, no such right existed.

4. **What rationale did the Court of Justice give for the recognition of direct effect?**

The Court listed the following rationale:

✓ EEC Treaty is more than an agreement which merely creates mutual obligations between the contracting states;
✓ The Community constitutes a new legal order of international law for the benefit of which the states have limited their sovereign rights;
✓ EEC law confers rights on individuals in addition to obligations.

In addition, ***Van Duyn*** is another important case. It is the first case establishing that directives are capable of having direct effect, because of the following reasons:

✓ Directive directly affects an individual is capable of creating direct rights for that individual;
✓ The only 'adequate legal remedy' available to an individual is the right to invoke the provisions of the Directive before the national courts. A decision to this effect would undoubtedly strengthen the legal protection of individual citizens in the national courts;
✓ EU Law empowers national courts to refer to the Court questions concerning the validity and interpretation of all acts of the Community institutions, without distinction, implies furthermore that these acts may be invoked by individuals in the national courts.

5. **What are the legal requirements for an article of an EU Treaty to have direct effect?**

The following requirements must be satisfied:

✓ Sufficiently clear and precise;
✓ Unconditional;

✓ Against whom may it be relied upon?

    the State ('vertical direct effect')

    and

    a private party ('horizontal direct effect')

6. **What is a Regulation? What are the legal requirements for an article of a Regulation to have direct effect?**

According to Article 288 of the TFEU, regulations, as a secondary legal source, are applicable in Member States and are legally binding. The following requirements must be satisfied:

✓ Sufficiently clear and precise;
✓ Unconditional;

✓ Against whom may it be relied upon?

    the State ('vertical direct effect')

    and

    a private party ('horizontal direct effect')

7. **Distinguish Directives from Regulations. What are the legal requirements for an article of a Directive to have direct effect?**

Directives, like regulations, are a secondary legal source in EU Law. However, whereas directives have to be implemented by Member States, regulations automatically become part of national law.

Directives are applicable only against states and emanation of state (only vertical direct effect), while regulations can be used against states, emanation of state or private parties (vertical as well as horizontal direct effect).

8. **What problems did the Court of Justice encounter in reaching the conclusion that Directives may have direct effect? In what ways were they resolved?**

- Article 288 of the TFEU leaves it to the Member State to implement the Directive.
- A Directive can directly affect as long as it meets the *Van Gend en Loos* criteria

    i) Sufficiently clear and precise;
    ii) Unconditional;

    - The implementation date has passed *(Ratti)*r

    and

    - Not implemented at all (*Ratti*); or
    - Partially or incorrectly implemented (*VNO*); or
    - Correctly implemented but not applied in a way that achieves the result sought (*Marks & Spencer plc*)

    iii) It can be only against the State ('vertical'). NOT against a private party ('horizontal')

9. **What significance does the concept of an 'emanation of the State' have for direct effect? How can an emanation of the State be identified using legal criteria?**

Directives can only have direct effect against an emanation of the State.

Current test to understand an emanation of the State:

- **Farrell v MIBI (2017)**

Rejected tripartite test

Reformulated bipartite test:

✓ Is a legal person governed by public law that is part of the State;

or

✓ Is subject to the authority or control of a public body;

or

✓ Is required by a public body to perform a task in the public interest for which it has special powers.

CASE STUDY:

Directive 2012/118 (fictitious) necessitated Member States taking steps to ensure the provision of amenities for those with mobility impairments in all transport facilities. The directive defines 'mobility impairment' as 'physical disability that adversely affects mobility'.

Member States were required to implement the directive by May 2014. Special Needs Ordinance ('the Ordinance') (fictitious), which came into force in November 2013. The Ordinance stated that lifts must be provided at Metro stations for all passengers in wheelchairs. In April 2015, Mila, who was 7 months pregnant and had back and pelvic pain related to her pregnancy, was prevented from accessing the lift in a Metro station. France implemented Directive 2012/118 by means of the Public Transport Facilities Act. The Metro station in question is run by a company founded fifty years ago following French legislation enacted for the provision of public transport. This legislation grants it various powers, including the authority to issue fines and make byelaws. The company operates under the auspices of the regional authority. Mila was prevented from using the lift during rush hour on the grounds that she was not in a wheelchair. Consequently, she had no alternative but to use the stairs, and fell as she went up the steps, breaking her ankle in the process.

Counsel Mila regarding whether the directive can in this case have direct effect in the relevant national courts under EU law.

1. **Van Gend en Loos criteria must be satisfied to say that there is a direct effect:**

   - **The Directive must be sufficiently clear and precise**

   Yes, it is sufficiently clear and precise here.

   - **It must be unconditional. Is the Directive unconditional?**

   Yes, it is unconditional.

   - **Did implementation date pass? (*Ratti*)**

   Implementation Deadline: May 2014

   Accident happened: April 2015

   Yes, implementation date was passed at the time of the accident.

   And

   - **Was the Directive implemented?**

     Three possibilities:

- Not implemented at all *(Ratti)*;
- Or correctly implemented but not applied by national authorities in a way that achieves the result sought *(Marks & Spencer plc)*;
- Or only partially and/or incorrectly implemented *(VNO)*.

Directive = Must have appropriate amenities for the mobility-impaired.

- Defined as 'physical impairment which reduces mobility'.

- Ordinance = Lifts only made available to wheelchair-bound travellers.

The French law does not cover other forms of reduced mobility. In other words, the Directive was partially and/or incorrectly implemented.

2. **Who will be against?**

Two possibilities:

It may be relied upon against the State ('vertical direct effect')

But <u>not</u> against a private individual ('horizontal direct effect')

- **Is the underground train station an emanation of the state?**

Application of *Farrell* test:

1) **Is a legal person governed by public law that is part of the State?**

   No

2) **Or is subject to the authority or control of a public body?**

   The company functions under the direction of the regional authority. Regional authority is an organ of the State.

3) **Or is required by a public body to perform a task in the public interest for which it has special powers?**

   Station operated by a company established by French legislature to provide public transport. The legislation provides the company with powers to issue penalty fines and to make bylaws.

   The station is an emanation of the state under either (2) or (3).

In conclusion, the mentioned Directive can have direct effect in the relevant national courts under EU law.

Important Case list:

Concept of an Emanation of the State

Farrell v Motor Insurers Bureau of Ireland (Case C-413/15) [2017] ECR I-000

Foster v British Gas plc. (No.2) [1991] 2 AC 306

Direct Effect

Marks & Spenser plc v Commissioners of Customs & Excise (Case C-62/00) [2002] ECR I-6325

NV Algemene Transport - en Expeditie Onderneming van Gend en Loos v Nederlandse Administratie der Belastingen (Case 26/62) [1963] ECR 1

Pubblico Ministero v Tullio Ratti (Case 148/78) [1980] 1 CMLR 96

Van Duyn v Home Office (Case 41/74) [1975] 1 CMLR 1

Verbond van Nederlandse Ondernemingen (VNO) v Inspecteur der Invoerrechten en Accijnzen (Case 51/76) [1977] ECR 113.

Supremacy (Direct Applicability)

Costa v E.N.E.L. (Case 6/64) [1964] ECR 585

CHAPTER III

ENFORCEMENT IN NATIONAL COURTS: INDIRECT EFFECT AND STATE LIABILITY

Learning Outcomes:

In this chapter, you should be able to understand:

- ✓ indirect effect and the interpretative obligation it entails;
- ✓ the limits to indirect effect;
- ✓ state liability and the requirements for it.

Questions and Answers:

1. **Define indirect effect.**

   National courts may utilize the provisions of directives to clarify the significance and breadth of national legislation.

2. **Which case originally established indirect effect?**

   The principle of indirect effect originated in the case of ***Von Colson***. Two female social workers applied for jobs at the Werl men's prison in Germany. They were not employed by the prison, with the jobs going to male applicants with fewer qualifications. Although a German labour court found there had been sex discrimination, it decided the Equal Treatment Directive did not necessitate a specific remedy. As a result, the only provision available to the court in German law was to award damages for actual loss, which in this case meant reimbursing transport expenses.

   a. **What was the rationale provided by the Court of Justice for the introduction of indirect effect?**

   The Court of Justice provided the following rationale:

   - ✓ Member states must achieve the result envisaged by the Directive (Article 288 of the TFEU).
   - ✓ Member states must take all appropriate measures to ensure Treaty obligations are fulfilled (Article 4(3) of the TEU).

b. What obligation did the Court of Justice place on the national courts of Member States in order to give indirect effect to EU law?

The obligation for national courts is clearly stated as follows: "…national courts are required to interpret their national law in the light of the wording and purpose of the Directive in order to achieve the result [envisaged by the Directive]…" (para. 26).

It should also be noted that it is up to national courts to decide how and to what degree to implement the Directive in national law:

"…It is for the national court to interpret and apply the legislation adopted for the implementation of the Directive in conformity with the requirements of Community law, **in so far as it is given discretion to do so under national law**" (para. 28) **(Bold added).**

3. **As a result of *Von Colson* case, please explain the following resulting questions:**

    a) Can indirect effect apply horizontally between private parties?

    Yes, indirect effect is available against a private party (***Harz***).

    b) Does indirect effect apply where the national law was not enacted to implement an EU measure?

    Yes, indirect effect applies whether the provisions in question were adopted before or after the Directive (***Marleasing***).

    c) What is the precise scope of 'in so far as it is given discretion to do so under national law'?

    No, when national law explicitly contradicts EU law there is no indirect effect. That is, if provisions in national law rule something out entirely, they may not be construed in a manner that accords with a directive (***Wagner Miret and Marleasing***).

4. **What is state liability?**

State liability permits a person to obtain compensation from a Member State when loss has been sustained on account of that Member State failing to fulfil its obligations under EU law.

5. **Which case originally established indirect effect?**

The case of ***Francovich and Bonifaci*** created the principle of state liability. The two applicants had not been paid the wages owing to them on account of the companies they worked for going bankrupt. Directive 80/987 seemed to be designed for such a situation. This directive stipulated that each Member State should set up institutions to ensure employees of companies that had gone bankrupt could be reimbursed for wages they had not been paid. However, Italy had not transposed the Directive and the deadline for its introduction had passed. Furthermore, the Commission had concluded that Italy had not fulfilled its obligations under EU law in not implementing the Directive. Since the applicants could not apply for compensation under a national law, they looked to the Directive for redress. Consequently, the Italian Court submitted the case to the Court of Justice.

a) What was the rationale provided by the Court of Justice for the introduction of indirect effect?

The Court of Justice provided the following rationale:

✓ Full effectiveness of Community rules would be impaired and the protection of the rights would be weakened if individuals were unable to obtain redress.

✓ Member States must take all appropriate measures to ensure Treaty obligations are fulfilled (Article 4(3) of the TEU).

b) Explain the principles laid down by the Court of Justice in *Francovich*.

Three requirements must be satisfied for the principle of state liability:

✓ The result prescribed by the Directive should entail the **grant of rights to individuals**;

✓ It should be possible to identify the **content of those rights** on the basis of the Directive;

✓ There must be **a causal link** between the breach and the loss/damage suffered.

6. **How has state liability developed in case of the joined cases of *Brasserie du Pêcheur and Factortame III (no 4)*? What were the requirements?**

In the ***Brasserie du Pêcheur and Factortame III (no 4)*** cases the extent of the principle was broadened and the circumstances for state liability were redefined. Brasserie du Pêcheur was a brewery in France. Its exports of beer to Germany were halted by the German government, leading to the company suing the German government for compensation for losses it had incurred. In Factortame III, Spanish fishermen claimed the UK Merchant Shipping Act of 1998 was not compatible with the Treaty since the Act stopped them operating in the UK waters on account of it stipulating that fishing vessels had to belong to British companies and be managed from the UK.

The Court held that state liability applies:

-   for any case in which a Member State breaches Community law whatever organ of the State (including a national legislature) was responsible for the breach even where a measure is directly effective
-   Where there is a wide discretion, the state is liable where three conditions must be satisfied:

    ✓ Measure intended to **confer rights** on individuals;
    ✓ Breach must be **sufficiently serious**;
    ✓ Direct **casual link** between the breach and the damage.

7. **When will a breach be sufficiently serious for the purpose of state liability?**

    When the Member State has **manifestly and gravely** disregarded the limits on its discretion *(Brasserie du Pêcheur)*, there will be a sufficiently serious breach.

    It should be noted that there will be an automatic breach if:

    ✓ The Member State had limited or no discretion; or
    ✓ The Member State took no steps to implement a Directive *(Dillenkofer)*.

CASE STUDY:

Directive 2012/118 (fictitious) necessitated Member States taking steps to ensure the provision of amenities for those with mobility impairments in all transport facilities. The directive defines 'mobility impairment' as 'physical disability that adversely affects mobility'.

Member States were required to implement the directive by May 2014. Special Needs Ordinance ('the Ordinance') (fictitious), which came into force in November 2013. The Ordinance stated that lifts must be provided at Metro stations for all passengers in wheelchairs. In April 2015, Mila, who was 7 months pregnant and had back and pelvic pain related to her pregnancy, was prevented from accessing the lift in a Metro station. France implemented Directive 2012/118 by means of the Public Transport Facilities Act. The Metro station in question is run by a company founded fifty years ago following

French legislation enacted for the provision of public transport. This legislation grants it various powers, including the authority to issue fines and make byelaws. The company operates under the auspices of the regional authority. Mila was prevented from using the lift during rush hour on the grounds that she was not in a wheelchair. Consequently, she had no alternative but to use the stairs, and fell as she went up the steps, breaking her ankle in the process.

Advise Mila as to whether or not they will be able to rely on indirect effect or state liability in order to obtain a remedy in their respective cases.

a-) Indirect effect principal was established in *Von Colson*. It applies in the following circumstances: <u>both</u> vertically *(Von Colson)* and horizontally *(Harz)*.

- **There are several limitations on indirect effect:**

Indirect effect principle can only be after the implementation deadline has passed.

Implementation Deadline: May 2014

Accident happened: April 2015

Deadline has passed at the time of this accident.

This principle must not determine or aggravate criminal liability

Criminal liability is irrelevant here.

- National courts must interpret "as far as possible" (*Marleasing*) as indirect effect principle required. But it will <u>not</u> be possible if the national law contradicts the Directive *(Wagner-Miret)*.
- Can a pregnant woman suffering from back and pelvic pain who would find it extremely difficult to use stairs be considered within the scope of the term 'wheelchair-bound travellers' as found in the Ordinance?

The national law does not contradict the Directive.
In conclusion, indirect effect is applicable in case of the claimant.

b-) With regards to the principle of state liability, this principle was established in *Francovich*.

- Involved failure to take any steps to implement
- In the question scenario, France has taken steps to implement (albeit inadequate steps)

State liability requirements were extended in ***Brasserie du Pêcheur SA/Factortame Ltd:***

Was the rule intended to confer rights on individuals?

Yes, it was. Confers right to have appropriate amenities for the mobility impaired.

Was the breach sufficiently serious?

In all probability it would be considered sufficiently serious in this case as the words 'reduced mobility' are explicitly broader than 'wheelchair-bound'. Furthermore, there are no reasonable grounds for France to justify its failure to implement the Directive in a proper way.

Was there a direct causal link between the breach and the damage?

Mila would not have been injured if she had been permitted to use the lift.

In conclusion, Mila would be allowed to ask for a compensation under the principle of state liability.

Important Case List:

Indirect Effect

Harz v Deutsche Tradax (Case 79/83) [1986] 2 CMLR 430

Marleasing SA v La Comercial Internacional de Alimentacion SA (Case C-106/89) [1992] 1 CMLR 305

Von Colson (Sabine) and Elisabeth Kamann v Land Nordrhein-Westfalen (Case 14/83) [1986] 2 CMLR 430

Wagner Miret (Teodoro) v Fondo de Grantia Salarial (Case C-334/92) [1996] 1 CMLR 889

State Liability

Brasserie du Pêcheur SA v Germany; R v Secretary of State for Transport, ex parte Dillenkofer and others v Germany (Joined cases C-178/94, C-179/94, C-188/94, C-189/94 and C-190/94) [1996] 3 CMLR 469

Factorame (Factortame III) (Joines Cases 46 & 48/93) [1996] 1 CMLR 889

Francovich (Andrea) and Another v Italian Republic (Cases 6/90 & 990) [1993] 2 CMLR 66

CHAPTER IV

FREE MOVEMENT OF GOODS: FISCAL BARRIERS

Learning Outcomes:

In this chapter, you should be able to understand:

- ✓ the definition of goods;
- ✓ the prohibition in Article 30 of the TFEU;
- ✓ which charges fall outside Article 30 of the TFEU;
- ✓ when a tax is prohibited under Article 110 of the TFEU.

Questions and Answers:

1. **What are goods?**

   "Products which can be valued in money and which are capable, as such, of forming the subject of commercial transactions" (*Commission v Italy – 'Art Treasures', p. 428*).

2. **Explain the difference between customs duties and charges having equivalent effect to a customs duty under Article 30 of the TFEU.**

   Article 30 states that

   > "Customs duties on imports and exports and charges having equivalent effect shall be prohibited between Member States. This prohibition shall also apply to customs duties of a fiscal nature."

   Customs duty is the charge applied to goods – both imports and exports – on the crossing of a border *(Art Treasures)*.

   Charges having equivalent effect to a customs duty (CEE) means that "any pecuniary charge, however small and whatever its designation and mode of application which is imposed unilaterally on domestic or foreign goods by reason of the fact that they cross a frontier and which is not a customs duty in the strict sense constitutes a charge having equivalent effect... even if it is not imposed for the benefit of the State, is not discriminatory or protective in effect and if the product on which the charge is imposed is not in competition with any domestic product" (**Commission v Italy - 'Statistical Levy', para. 9**).

3. **When will a fiscal charge fall outside of Article 30 of the TFEU?**

There is no CEE in the following circumstances:

a) **Internal tax**: This charge does not come under Article 30. Rather, it comes under Article 110 **(Alfons Lütticke)**.

b) **Payment for a service**: For instance, if mandatory veterinary inspections of animal products entering a member state incur a charge, this service will not be considered as CEE. However, what is important is that the service provided should be of benefit to the importer. In the event that the service in question is for the general public, it will be considered CEE **(Customs Warehouses)**.

c) **Attached to an EU inspection**: If an inspection is necessary under EU Law to facilitate the free movement of goods, a charge levied by a Member State for an inspection is not considered CEE **(Animal Inspections)**.

d) **International inspection**: Inspection fee introduced for all member states by an international treaty that promotes the free movement of goods. This is also true for charges for inspections that come about as a consequence of rules introduced by international treaties **(Commission v Netherlands)**.

4. **What is an internal tax under Article 110 of the TFEU?**

Internal tax means that "…it relates to a general system of internal dues applied systematically to categories of products in accordance with objective criteria irrespective of the origin of the products" **(Commission v France - 'Levy on Reprographic Machinery', para. 14)**. But Article 110 prohibits discriminatory and protectionist taxation.

5. **Why are internal taxes more acceptable than custom duties and charges having equivalent effect to a customs duty?**

Internal taxes are seen as an issue of national sovereignty. Furthermore, such taxes need not hinder the free movement of goods.

6. **How does the Court of Justice determine whether or not products are similar for the purpose of Article 110(1) of the TFEU?**

Article 110(1) applies to similar products. There are two golden requirements for Article 110(1):

✓ The imported and domestic products must be similar;

✓ Taxation must not discriminate against the imports.

7. How will you know whether the products are similar?

Similar characteristics must be present at the same phase of marketing or production. Moreover, such products must address the same requirements as regards consumers *(Casis de Dijon)*.

Such products need not be absolutely identical, but their uses must be similar and of equivalent quality *(Spirits)*.

8. When will a discriminatory tax be permitted?

There are two types of discrimination:

- **Direct Discrimination:** The member state treats domestic goods more favourable than imported goods in terms of its origin ('in law') as well as in reality ('in fact'). Direct discrimination will not be permitted *(Regenerated Oil)*.

- **Indirect Discrimination:** The member state's law does not make any distinction between domestic and imported goods in terms of its origin, but in reality ('in fact'), taxation targets imported goods. Such discrimination may be allowed if it is justifiable on an objective non-discriminatory basis *(Humblot; Commission v Greece)*. In the case of *Chemial Farmaceutici*, the Court of Justice held that

  i) Tax must differentiate between products on the basis of **objective criteria**;

  ii) Must pursue **economic policy objectives** compatible with EU law;

  iii) **Detailed rules** must avoid discrimination.

9. When will differences in taxation between non-similar products be prohibited under Article 110(2) of the TFEU?

Article 110(2) states that

> "No Member State shall impose on the products of other Member States **any internal taxation** of such a nature as to afford indirect protection to other products" **(Bold added)**.

Article 110(2) does not permit tax which indirectly protects other goods to be levied on imported goods. In other words, this Article applies to non-similar goods which are in competition with domestic good partially or indirectly or potentially *(Commission v France - 'Spirits')*.

If taxation reduces **(Even potential)** the sales of imported goods while benefiting similar domestic products, it is considered unlawful *(Commission v Belgium)*.

CASE STUDY:

A German couple, Alex and his wife Anna, both own businesses. Alex's business sells spare parts and accessories for automobiles in Germany. One item he distributes is gaskets for engines, which are made from various materials. The German government has introduced a charge on gaskets that are not manufactured from recycled materials in order to encourage the use of recycled material. The same charge is also applied to all imported gaskets, since it is not possible to verify whether they are manufactured from recycled materials or not. While it would be possible for Alex to purchase cheaper gaskets in other Member States, the additional charge makes them more expensive than gaskets produced in Germany.

Anna's business imports plug-in electric air fresheners from France to Germany. The German Tax Office applies a charge to all imported electric air fresheners. This charge is used to fund the compilation of data on these air fresheners, which is then provided to importers for their benefit.

Give Alex and Anna advice regarding the legality of the above-mentioned provisions under EU law on fiscal barriers to free trade.

Issues:

    1-) Charge on imported gaskets

    2-) Charge on fresheners

Application:

1. Charge on imported gaskets

- **Does Article 30 or Article 110 involve?**
  Cannot be both (*Lütticke*).

Imposed on gaskets manufactured in Germany as well as on imported gaskets.

Therefore:

Part of a system of dues which apply to domestic and imported goods =

Internal tax (Article 110 involves).

- **Does Article 110(1) apply?**

  Yes, because they have similar characteristics and meet the same needs *(Rewe-Zentrale)*.

- **Is there direct discrimination?**

  Yes

- **Can you justify direct discrimination?**

  No, direct discrimination will not be justified.

  (E.g. Commission v Italy – 'Regenerated Oil').

2. **Charge on fresheners**

- **Does Article 30 or Article 110 involve?**

  Article 30

- **Is this charge a customs duty?**

  No

- **Is it CEE?**

  Will be if charge for crossing the frontier *('Statistical Levy')*

  But not if

  ✓ Falls under *Commission v Germany* situations

    Application to the facts:

  ✓ Is it payment for a service?

    No

  ✓ Analogous to *'Statistical Levy'* case

In conclusion, this fictitious case is similar to *Statistical Levy* case; therefore it will be treated as a CEE. It will be a violation of Article 30.

Important Case List:

Customs Duty or Charges Having Equivalent Effect

Commission v Belgium (Case 132/82) [1983] ECR 1649 (Customs Warehouses)

Commission v Germany (Case 18/87) [1990] 1 CMLR 561 (Animal Inspections)

Commission v Italy (Case 24/68) [1971] CMLR 611 (Statistical Levy)

Commission v Netherlands (Case 89/76) [1977] ECR 1355

Definition of Goods

Commission v Italy (Case 7/68) [1969] CMLR 1 (Art Treasures)

Internal Taxation

Alfons Lütticke GmbH v Hauptzollamt Saarlouis (Case 57/65) [1966] ECR 205

Chemial Farmaceutici SpA v DAF SpA (Case 140/79) [1981] 3CMLR 350

Commission v France (Case 90/79) [1981] 3 CMLR 1 (Reprographic Machinery)

Commission v Greece (Case 132/88) [1991] 3 CMLR 1

Commission v Italy (Case 21/79) [1980] 2 CMLR 613 (Regenerated Oil)

Humblot v Directeur des Services Fiscaux (Case 112/84) [1986] 2 CMLR 338

Similar Goods

Commission v Denmark (Case 106/84) [1987] 2 CMLR 278

Rewe-Zentrale AG v Bundesmonopolverwaltung für Branntwein (Case 120/78) [1979] ECR 649 (Casis de Dijon)

Non-Similar Goods

Commission v Belgium (Case 356/85) [1988] 3 CMLR 277

Commission v France (Case 168/78) [1981] 2 CMLR 631(Spirits)

CHAPTER V

FREE MOVEMENT OF GOODS: NON-FISCAL BARRIERS

Learning Outcomes:

In this chapter, you should be able to understand:

- ✓ the prohibitions on quantitative restrictions and on MEQRs under Article 34 of the TFEU (imports)
- ✓ the difference between distinctly applicable and indistinctly applicable MEQRs;
- ✓ the defences to Article 34 of the TFEU;
- ✓ when selling arrangements fall outside Article 34 of the TFEU.

Questions and Answers:

1. **What is the key article for non-fiscal barriers? Who is bound by Articles 34 and 35 of the TFEU?**

   The key articles are Article 34, 35 and 36 of the TFEU.

   Public bodies (e.g. legislative, executive and judiciary) and Quasi Public bodies (e.g. Royal Pharmaceutical Society, Bar Society, Solicitors Regularity Authority) within member states are bound by Article 34 and 35. Entirely private organisations and individuals are beyond the boundaries of these Articles.

2. **What are the types of non-fiscal barriers? Explain the difference between quantitative restrictions and measures having equivalent effect to a quantitative restriction (MEQRs) under Article 34 of the TFEU.**

   There are two types:

   - ✓ Quantitative Restrictions (QR);
   - ✓ Measures having equivalent effect to a quantitative restriction (MEQR)

   QR means that "[t]he prohibition on quantitative restrictions covers measures which amount to a total or partial restraint of, according to the circumstances, imports, exports or goods in transit" *(Geddo, para. 7)*. For instance, a ban or a quota on imports are an example of QR.

MEQR means that a plethora of provisions can be considered hidden barriers to trade. For instance, national regulations may impose requirements of specific packaging in order for it to be sold to the public. The Court of Justice held in the case of *Dassonville*: "All trading rules enacted by Member States which are capable of hindering, directly or indirectly, actually or potentially, intra-Community trade" (para. 5). This definition extended the concepts of MEQRs.

3.   What are the types of MEQRs?

There are two types of MEQRs:

✓   Distinctly;
✓   Indistinctly.

Distinctly MEQRs do not have equal force for domestic and imported goods. These provisions disadvantage imports since they hinder or make the importing procedure more expensive compared to similar domestic products. An example of this is the imposition of unreasonable extra measures on imported goods. Another example is the limiting of channels by which goods are imported. Another method is for national rules to discriminate directly in favour of domestic products *(Irish Souveniers)*.

Indistinctly MEQRs are valid for both domestic and imported goods without distinction. However, in practice they may still be prejudicial towards imported goods *(Cinetheque)*.

4.   What is presumption of mutual recognition? What impact has Cassis de Dijon had?

Indistinctly MEQRs was confirmed in the case of *Cassis de Dijon*. An importer wished to buy the liqueur 'Casisis de Dijon', made in France, and import it to sell in Germany. German law stipulates that such liqueurs must have a minimum alcohol content of 25 per cent. However, the alcohol content of this liqueur is between 15 and 20 per cent. Hence, importing it into Germany was not allowed.

This case established two important principles:

- **Presumption of mutual recognition:** The presumption is derived from the following statement by the Court:

  "There is therefore no valid reason why, provided that they have been lawfully produced and marketed in one of the Member States, alcoholic beverages should not be introduced into any other Member State; the sale of such products may not be subject to a legal prohibition on the marketing of beverages with an alcohol content lower than the limit set by the national rules" (para. 14).

This quotation means that if a product is lawfully produced and marketed in one Member State, it is entitled to be sold in another Member State.

This principle in essence prevents a 'dual burden' being imposed on the imported goods, as these products will need to meet the standards in the Member State where the product is produced as well as in the Member State into which the product is being imported. The rules will probably be different in the two countries, leading to additional burdens and increased costs. Hence, this principle is crucial as regards preventing a dual burden situation for imported goods. The imported goods should only be required to comply with the rules of their home Member State.

- **Mandatory requirements:** The Court also underlined an additional defence on the top of Article 36 of the TFEU derogations. Please note that this defence is only available in relation to indistinctly applicable MEQRs. The Court stated in the case of ***Dassonville*** that:

  "In the absence of a Community system guaranteeing for consumers the authenticity of a product's designation of origin, if a Member State takes measures to prevent unfair practices in this connexion, it is however subject to the condition that these measures should be reasonable and that the means of proof required should not act as a hindrance to trade between Member States and should, in consequence, be accessible to all Community nationals" (para. 6).

5. What is the defense mechanism under Article 36 of the TFEU?

Article 36 contains grounds for the Member State regarding barriers to the free movement of goods. Six reasons are given which a Member State may use to justify the restriction: public morality; public policy; public security; the protection of health and life of humans, animals or plants; the protection of national treasures possessing artistic, historic or archaeological value; or the protection of industrial and commercial property.

6. What is a selling arrangement?

A selling arrangement refers to provisions governing who sells a product and the circumstances regarding when, where and how the seller does it.

7. **How does the Court of Justice distinguish between a selling arrangement and an MEQR?**

According to **Keck** case, the difference is as follows:

MEQR: Obstacles resulting from requirements to be met by imports e.g. designation, form, size, weight, composition, presentation, labelling, packaging (i.e. product requirements and characteristics).

Selling Arrangements: Not MEQRs as long as the following conditions have to be satisfied:

- **It must apply to all relevant traders operating in national territory and**
- **It must affect the marketing of domestic and imported goods in the same in the same manner, in law and in fact.**

CASE STUDY:

The government in Germany has introduced measures aiming to enhance commercial practice.

Alex is a distributor of automobile spare parts and accessories in Germany. A delivery of children's safety seats he had arranged to import from Belgium was confiscated by Germany authorities on the grounds that the seats were in boxes that did not display a warning required by German law to the effect that 'all children's safety seats are not for self-assembly and should be fitted by a trained car mechanic'. Germany is the only country to have this safety requirement.

The German government has launched an advertising campaign on TV involving Peter Owen, a motoring journalist who is also an environmentalist, to promote its message that 'cars are bad for the environment'. Due to the success of this campaign in reducing car sales in Germany, Alex is selling many fewer spare parts. However, his sales are down at a similar rate in both domestic and imported items.

Give Alex advice regarding the legality of the measures referred to above under EU law.

Issues:

1-) Confiscation of seats;

2-) TV advertising campaign.

Application:

1-) Confiscation of seats

Does QR or MEQR involve?

It is not QR because this restriction is not a direct restraint on quantity of imports *(Geddo test)*.

It is **MEQR** because this restriction is capable of hindering, directly or indirectly, actually or potentially, intra-community trade *(Dassonville)*.

What type of MEQRs apply?

It is indistinctly applicable MEQRs.

Can this restriction be justified?

Two potential defence options you can use:

Mandatory requirement?

Most realistic ground: Consumer protection?

Derogations Under Article 36?

Most realistic ground: Protection of health and life of humans?

> This potential ground needs to involve a fundamental interest of the state; and
>
> It is interpreted very strictly. Rarely succeeds.

Is confiscation necessary?

No, it will not be proportionate to confiscate them.

In conclusion, it is very unlikely for the Court to accept this derogation. Overall, there will be a violation of Article 34.

2-) TV advertising campaign

Does QR or MEQRs involve?

No, it is not QR because it is not a direct restraint on quantity of imports *(Geddo test)*.

MEQR?

May be depending on whether it is a selling arrangement or not.

The **Keck** test should be applied in order to understand whether it is a selling arrangement:

Does it relate to selling arrangements rather than physical requirements?

Yes

= Restriction on marketing of automobile spare parts and accessories, not on its physical characteristics

✓ **Does it apply to all relevant traders in the national territory?**

Yes

✓ **Does it affect domestic and imported goods the same in law and in fact? In other words, is it more difficult for imported goods to break into German market?**

Alex losing sales equally on domestic and imported goods.

In conclusion, it is a selling arrangement. Therefore, it is not MEQR.

Important Case List:

Defences

Conegate Ltd v Commissioners of Customs and Excise (Case 121/85) [1986] ECR 1007

Procureur du Roi v Benoit and Gustave Dassonville (Case 8/74) [1974] ECR 837

Walter Rau Lebensmittelwerke v Smedt PvbA (Case 261/81) [1982] ECR 3961

Measures having equivalent effect to a quantitative restriction (MEQRs)

Cinéthèque SA and others v Fédération Nationale des Cinémas Français (Joined cases 60 and 61/84) [1985] ECR 2605

Commission v Ireland (Case 113/80) [1981] ECR 01625 (Irish Souveniers)

Commission v Ireland (Case 249/81) [1982] ECR 4005

Firma Denkavit Futtermittel GmbH v Minister fur Ernahgrung (Case 251/78) [1979] ECR 3369

Procereur du Roi v Benoit and Gustave Dassonville (Case 8/74) [1974] ECR 837

Rewe-Zentrale AG v Bundesmonopolverwaltung für Branntwein (Case 120/78) [1979] ECR 649 (Casis de Dijon)

Quantitate Restrictions (QR)

Geddo v Ente Nazionale Risi (Case 2/73) [1974] 1 CMLR 13

Selling Arrangements

Criminal Proceedings against Keck and Mithouard (Cases C-267 & C-268/91) [1993] ECR I-6097

CHAPTER VI

FREE MOVEMENT OF PERSONS: ENTRY AND RESIDENCE

Learning Outcomes:

In this chapter, you should be able to understand:

- ✓ the concepts of a worker, a Union citizen and a family member;
- ✓ their basic rights to enter and reside in a Member State;
- ✓ the further rights of residence which EU law provides;
- ✓ the public service exemption;
- ✓ the derogations.

Questions and Answers:

1. **Who is a worker under Article 45 of the TFEU?**

   Article 45 does not give a definition. This article only states that "Freedom of movement for workers shall be secured within the Union" (Article 45(1)).

   In the *Lawrie-Blum* case (para. 12), the Court of Justice held identified three essential criteria to be a worker:

   - ✓ to perform services;
   - ✓ to work for and under the direction of another person; and
   - ✓ to receive remuneration in return.

2. **What is an economic activity?**

   In the case of *Levin*, the Court of Justice held that

   > "...those rules cover only the pursuit of effective and genuine activities, to the exclusion of activities on such a small scale as to be regarded as purely marginal and ancillary" (para. 17).

   This case extended the definition of worker. In other words, part time employment is also deemed an adequate term to define someone as a worker if the activity is an effective and genuine economic activity.

In the case of **Steymann,** the Court found that work connected to a community's commercial activities constituted a genuine and effective economic activity. The applicant, Mr Steymann, worked for a religious community in the Netherlands. In return, he receives a pocket money, accommodation and food. This case underlines that remuneration does not only include salary. It might cover accommodation and food etc.

3. Is a job seeker accepted as a worker?

The free movement of workers referred to in Article 45 of the TFEU does not only include people engaged in employment. The right to accept a job offer (Article 45(3)(a)) and the right to remain in a Member State after having worked in that State is also included, subject to conditions enshrined in regulations drawn up by the Commission (Article 45(3)(d)). In the case of **Antonissen,** the Court of Justice stated clearly that as long as a person is an effective and genuine job seeker, s/he will be accepted as a worker for a reasonable period. In this case, 6 months was accepted as reasonable time because the applicant showed an evidence that continuing to seek employment and had a genuine chance of being engaged.

4. Who is a union citizen and a family member?

According to Article 20(1) of the TFEU, a union citizen is defined as follows: "every person holding the nationality of a Member State shall be a citizen of the Union."

According to Article 2 of Directive 2004/38, family members are as follows: spouse; registered partner; direct descendants under the age of 21 or dependent and dependent direct relatives in the ascending line.

Article 3 of the Directive also grants the status of 'beneficiaries' to two other categories of people:

a) any other family members, irrespective of their nationality, not falling under the definition in point 2 of Article 2 who, in the country from which they have come, are dependants or members of the household of the Union citizen having the primary right of residence, or where serious health grounds strictly require the personal care of the family member by the Union citizen;

b) the partner with whom the Union citizen has a durable relationship, duly attested.

It is important to note that beneficiaries are not considered family members within the meaning of Article 2(2). Nevertheless, Article 3 puts a responsibility on the Member State to ensure the entry and residence of beneficiaries of the Union citizen, in line with its national legislation.

5. What are the basic rights under Directive 2004/38?

Every union citizen and his/her family member has the following rights: The right to entry; the right to residence up to 3 months; the right to residence over 3 months.

6. Explain the right to entry

Union citizens and their family members are able to travel from the home Member State and enter the host Member State merely by proffering a valid passport or identification card (Article 4 and 5 of Directive). However, in the event the family member of the Union citizen is a non-EU national, a visa may still be needed to enter (Article 5(2) and 5(4) of Directive).

7. Explain the right to residence

- **Up to three months:** Union citizens and family members may stay for a period up to 3 months simply by holding a valid passport or identity card (Article 6 of Directive). If they become an unreasonable burden on the social assistance system of the host Member State (Article 14(1) of Directive), they will not retain this right.
- **Over three months:** According to Article 7(1) of the Directive, Union citizens must satisfy one of the following conditions to stay in the host Member State more than three months:

   (a) To be a worker or self-employed; **or**

   (b) To have sufficient resources not to become a burden on the social assistance system of the host Member State and to have comprehensive sickness insurance cover; **or**

   (c) To enrol as a student at a private or public establishment and to have comprehensive sickness insurance; **or**

   (d) Family member accompanying or joining Union citizen who satisfies the conditions referred to in points (a), (b) or (c).

Article 7(2) states that

   "the right to residence provided for in paragraph 1 shall extend to family members who are not nations of a Member State, accompanying or joining the Union citizen in the host Member State, provided that such Union citizen satisfies the conditions referred to in 1(a), (b) or (c)."

Article 16 of the Directive states that

"Union citizens who have resided legally for a continuous period of five years in the host Member State shall have the right of permanent residence there."

This is the rule which applies for union citizens as well as their family members.

8. How to retain a right of residence?

If a separation of married or registered partner ensues, the rights of a Non-EU spouse or partner will not be affected by this separation unless the marriage has been dissolved.

In the event of divorce, Article 13(2) of the Directive permits non-EU family members to retain residential rights:

(a) prior to initiation of the divorce or annulment proceedings or termination of the registered partnership referred to in point 2(b) of Article 2, the marriage or registered partnership has lasted at least three years, including one year in the host Member State; or

(b) by agreement between the spouses or the partners referred to in point 2(b) of Article 2 or by court order, the spouse or partner who is not a national of a Member State has custody of the Union citizen's children; or

(c) this is warranted by particularly difficult circumstances, such as having been a victim of domestic violence while the marriage or registered partnership was subsisting; or

(d) by agreement between the spouses or partners referred to in point 2(b) of Article 2 or by court order, the spouse or partner who is not a national of a Member State has the right of access to a minor child, provided that the court has ruled that such access must be in the host Member State, and for as long as is required.

Article 12 of the Directive deals with residence rights of family members in the event of the death or departure of the Union citizen. There are conditions to this right. For instance, Article 12(3) states that "The Union citizen's departure from the host Member State or his/her death shall not entail loss of the right of residence of his/her children or of the parent who has actual custody of the children, irrespective of nationality, if the children reside in the host Member State and are enrolled at an educational establishment, for the purpose of studying there, until the completion of their studies."

9. What are the derogations?

Article 45(3) of the TFEU allows restrictions to be imposed on the freedom of movement for workers on the grounds of public policy, public security or public health.

It is important to note that the personal behaviour of the individual in question must present a real, current and sufficiently grave threat to the fundamental interests of society *(Bouchereau)*. A criminal record is not on its own sufficient reason for deportation. Furthermore, deportation must be proportionate. In other words, such steps must be in line with fundamental human rights *(Rutili)*.

10. What is a public service exemption?

Article 45(4) of the TFEU notes that there is an exception as regards the provisions of Article 45 in that they do not apply to public service employment. That is, Member States have the right to maintain full sovereignty in public service appointments and discriminate in favour of their own nationals. This is on account of the possibility of issues of security and loyalty to the State arising in the event of non-nationals being employed *(Sotgiu)*.

Nevertheless, the Court of Justice has used this exemption by interpreting it narrowly. The Court found in the *Public Employees* case:

"a series of posts which involve direct or indirect participation in the exercise of powers conferred by public law and duties designed to safeguard the general interests of the state or of other public authorities. Such posts in fact presume on the part of those occupying them the existence of a special relationship of allegiance to the state and reciprocity of rights and duties which form the foundation of the bond of nationality." (para. 10).

CASE STUDY:

Anna is a German woman who came to Paris with her 18-year-old son Tom. She is married to Alex, a Brazilian citizen. They got married four years ago and lived in Portugal for two years. After a short time, Anna found an office job.

An Immigration official stopped Anna and asked her if she had sufficient funds to support her and her family for a year. The official also asked her to provide proof of the offer of work and questioned her about Tom and Alex saying they were not welcome on account of having no funds. The official eventually allowed them to enter France for three months.

Anna began work at an accountancy firm but local immigration officials contacted her and said that her residence was only until the end of term.

Nine months after arriving in France, Anna found out that Alex had been having affair and Alex moved out of the apartment they had rented.

Tom has applied for various jobs since arriving in France, but has not been successful. After being arrested for a public order offence at a demonstration he has been threatened with deportation. He has a criminal record having been found guilty in Portugal of throwing a brick through a window during a demonstration. He was fined by the Portuguese court.

Advise Anna, Tom and Alex of their rights, if any, under EU law relating to the free movement of persons.

Issues:

Anna:

- ✓ Asked to demonstrate sufficient funds and proof of job offer
- ✓ Only given leave to enter for three months. Later told that she can only reside until the end of the term

Tom:

- ✓ Only given leave to enter for 3 months
- ✓ The effect of his search for work
- ✓ Threatened with deportation

Alex:

- ✓ Only given leave to enter for 3 months
- ✓ Retention of his residence

Application:

1-) Entry into France

- **Anna: German citizen**
  Is a **Union Citizen**.

- **Tom: German citizen?**

if so, is a **Union Citizen**.

> – **If he is not a German citizen, is it possible to define him as a direct descendant under 21?**

Yes, he is a **family member in any event**.

- **Alex: Brazilian citizen**

Is a **Non-EU Citizen**, but he is a family member because of a spouse of Anna.

All can enter the host Member State.

2-) Residence in France

- **Up to 3 months:**
  - Anna, Tom and Alex have right of residence (Article 6). Therefore, Anna cannot be asked to demonstrate sufficient funds and proof of job offer.
- **Over three months:**
  - Anna: Right of residence if:
  ✓ a worker (Article 7(1)(a)) or
  ✓ has sufficient resources and comprehensive sickness insurance cover (Article 7(1)(b))

Anna is a worker (a teacher) *(Lawrie-Blum and Kempf)*. **Therefore, she can stay in France more than 3 months.**

- **Alex:** He is a family member. It depends on Anna satisfying Article 7(1)(a) or (b).

He can also stay in France with Anna.

- **Tom:** Also dependent on Anna satisfying Article 7(1)(a) or (b) unless he is a Union citizen fulfilling Article 7(1)(a), (b) or (c)

Tom is a job seeker. Therefore, he will be accepted as a worker under Article 45. Article 14(4)(b) of Directive 2004/38 cannot expel Union citizen seeking employment so long as:

  o he can provide evidence that he is doing so and
  o he has a genuine chance of being engaged

3-) Can Tom be deported?

Article 45(3) of the TFEU

> public policy,
> public security or
> public health

Article 27(1) of Directive 2004/38 extends these grounds to

Union Citizen and Family Members.

Tom is a family member of a Union citizen. Therefore, he is subjected to Article 27(1).

- **Which possible ground might be applicable?**

  Public Policy

- **Will the deportation be justifiable? Does it proportionate to deport him when pros and cons are compared?**

  In favour of deportation:

✓ Previous criminal convictions do not in themselves constitute grounds for taking such measures (Article 27(2)).
✓ Length of residence (Article 28(1)).
    In France for relatively short period of time
✓ Social and cultural integration (Article 28(1)).
    Unlikely in such short period

Against deportation:

✓ **Does conduct represent a genuine, present and sufficiently serious threat affecting one of the fundamental interests of society?** (Article 27(2))

Only arrested. Not convicted of the offence.

✓ **Was offence serious enough in any event?**
No
✓ **Will this deportation separate him from his family?**

Must take into account family situation (Article 28(1))

Relevant that removal from State where close family members are living is breach of Article 8 of the European Convention on Human Rights (ECHR) unless justified *(Orfanopoulos and Oliveri v Land Baden-Württemberg)*

He will not be deported because of no proportionality.

4-) Does Alex retain in France after separation?

Directive 2004/38 does not state anything on separation. But, the case-law states:

✓ Family member is not required to live permanently with Union citizen;
✓ But must live in the same member state;
✓ The rights of a spouse will remain unaffected by separation *(Diatta)*.

> **Alex retains right to reside in France.**
> **If Alex and Anna get divorced, what will be happen with Alex?**

Article 13(2) states that non-EU family member will retain right of reside if:

a) the marriage or registered partnership has lasted at least three years, including one year in the host Member State; or

(b) the spouse or partner who is not a national of a Member State has custody of the Union citizen's children; or

(c) warranted by particularly difficult circumstances, such as domestic violence; or

(d) the right of access to a minor child, provided that the court has ruled that such access must be in the host Member State, and for as long as is required.

Alex married Anna four years ago. Therefore, he can retain in France.

Important Case List:

Defining a worker

Deborah Lawrie-Blum v Land Baden-Wurttemberg (Case 66/85) [1987] 3 CMLR 389

Steymann v Staatssecretaris van Justitie (Case 196/87) [1988] ECR 6159

Derogations

Orfanopoulos and Oliveri v Land Baden-Württemberg (Cases C-482/01) [2004] ECR I-5257

Rutili v Minister for the Interior (Case 36/75) [1975] ECR 1219.

Effective and Genuine Economic Activity

Levin v Staatssecretaris van Justitie (Case 53/81) [1982] 2 CMLR 454

Job seeker

R *v Immigration Appeal Tribunal, ex parte Antonissen (Case 292/89) [1991] ECR I-745*

Public Service Exemption

Commission v Belgium ('Public Employees') (Case 149/79) [1980] ECR 3881

Sotgiu v Deutsche Bundespost (Case 152/73) [1974] ECR 153

Separation and Divorce

Diatta v Land Berlin (Case 267/83) [1985] ECR 567

CHAPTER VII

FREE MOVEMENT OF PERSONS: EMPLOYMENT, SOCIAL & EDUCATIONAL RIGHTS

Learning Outcomes:

In this chapter, you should be able to understand:

- ✓ relevant employment rights;
- ✓ relevant social rights;
- ✓ relevant educational rights;
- ✓ the effect of Union citizenship on these rights.

Questions and Answers:

1. **Explain employment rights of Union citizens under Article 45(2) of the TFEU**

   Article 45(2) states that

   > "Such freedom of movement shall entail the abolition of any discrimination based on nationality between workers of the Member States as regards employment, remuneration and other conditions of work and employment."

   Article 45(3) adds that this also includes the right 'to accept offers of employment actually made'.

2. **Explain employment rights of Union citizens under Regulation 492/2011**

   The fundamentals are elaborated in more detail by Regulation 492/2011. Section 1 of the Regulation (Articles 1 to 6) deals with issues regarding eligibility for employment and access to employment. Section 2 of the Regulation (Articles 7 to 10) deals with the question of equality of treatment after a worker has found a job.

   For instance, Article 3 prohibits Member States:

   - ✓ Introducing discriminatory restrictions or rules on:

- **Applications and proposals; or**
- **Entitlement to accept and seek work.**

✓ Other conditions and measures that have the purpose or consequence of preventing non-nationals taking up employment *(Angonese)*.

However, this article does not affect conditions regarding competence in language necessary on account of the type of position in question *(Groener)*.

Article 7 emphasises the significance of treating employees equally as regards nationality concerning working conditions, in particular:

- **Remuneration;**
- **Dismissal;**
- **Becoming unemployed;**
- **Reinstatement or**
- **Re-employment *(Sotgiu)*.**

3. Explain employment rights of family members

Article 23 of Directive 2004/38 states that

"Irrespective of nationality, the family members of a Union citizen who have the right of residence or the right of permanent residence in a Member State shall be entitled to take up employment or self-employment there" *(Gül)*.

4. Explain social advantages/rights

Article 7(2) of Regulation 492/2011 stipulates that an employee who is a citizen of a Member State "shall enjoy the same social and tax advantages as national workers".

Social advantages include childbirth loans, income allowance, funeral expenses benefit and so on. These benefits must be awarded due to status as employee or on account of the individual being resident on the national territory *(Even)*.

Members of a worker's family can indirectly qualify for the right under Article 7(2) *(Cristini)*.

Article 20 of the TFEU taken together with Article 18 also emphasises that citizens of the EU are entitled to equal treatment as regards having access to social assistance *(Cowan)*.

It should be noted that the host Member State shall not be obliged to confer entitlement to social assistance during the first three months of residence of a Union citizen (Article 24(2) of Directive 2004/38).

5. Explain education rights

Article 7(3) of Regulation 492/11 safeguards the right to education as follows: "He shall also, by virtue of the same right and under the same conditions as national workers, have access to training in vocational schools and retraining centres."

The children of workers with the same right of entitlement to general education, apprenticeship and vocational training courses as nationals of the host Member State (Article 10 of Regulation 492/11).

Please note that maintenance and training grants were accepted as social advantages within the meaning of Article 7(2) of Regulation 492/2011.

6. Difference between vocational schools and vocational training

Vocational schools are "establishments which provide only instruction interposed between periods of employment or else closely connected with employment, particularly during apprenticeships" *(Brown)*.

Vocational trainings are "any form of education which prepares for a qualification for a particular profession, trade or employment or which provides the necessary training and skills for such a profession, trade or employment...whatever the age and the level of training of the pupils or students, and even if the training programme includes an element of general education" *(Gravier)*.

Universities are accepted as vocational training *(Blaizot)*.

7. Explain discrimination

Article 45(2) of the TFEU prohibits discrimination as follows: "Such freedom of movement shall entail the abolition of any discrimination based on nationality between workers of the Member States as regards employment, remuneration and other conditions of work and employment."

There are two types of discrimination: direct or indirect.

Direct discrimination is prohibited in any circumstances. It occurs when workers from other Member States receive less favourable treatment than citizens of the host Member State *(Commission v France)*.

Indirect discrimination can be justified as long as there is an objective reason. This occurs in a situation when an employment condition is impartial regarding nationality, but when implemented affects non-national workers more profoundly than nationals. For instance, in the case of **Groener**, she applied for a job as part-time lecturer in art at a college in Ireland. However, she was unable to get the job on account of not possessing a language certificate in the Irish language. The Court of Justice found that the language condition for the position was justified on account of a policy of promoting Irish Gaelic, one of the official languages of Ireland, to enhance national identity and culture.

CASE STUDY:

Max is a Bulgarian citizen, married to a Russian citizen, Maria. They have a four-year-old son called James. They used to live in Bulgaria but moved to Germany to look for work. Max soon found a part-time job as a cashier in a local supermarket, but it is not a well-paid job. As for Maria, she managed to find a full-time office job.

Max and Maria sought childcare for James. A German neighbour suggested a local nursery where his daughter went. When they asked the nursery, they were told that only children with a German parent or a parent with a permanent right to remain were accepted on account of the nursery being funded by the local municipality.

Max also has a daughter from a previous marriage. She is twenty years old and called Chris. She went to Germany to stay with her father and received an offer to study at the Academy of Modern Dance in Berlin. But when she applied for a grant the application was rejected on the grounds of her Bulgarian citizenship. According to German law, only German citizens may obtain these grants.

Give advice to Max, Maria and Chris regarding any rights they may have under EU law pertaining to free movement. Information about their rights in Germany should be included in this advice.

Issues:

- ✓ Local childcare nursery place;
- ✓ Educational grant.

Application:

1-) Local childcare nursery place

- **Problem under German law =**

  Not German nationals and

  Have no right to permanent residence

- **Article 7(2) of Regulation 492/2011**

  A worker who is a national of a Member State "shall enjoy the same social and tax advantages as national workers."

- **Is either parent a worker who is a Member State national?**

  Yes, Max is a Bulgarian citizen.

Will a nursery place constitute a social advantage falling within Article7(2)?

- Includes all social and tax advantages, whether or not attached to the contract of employment *(Cristini)*
- Those generally granted to workers because of
  - ✓ their objective status as workers or
  - ✓ their residence on the national territory *(Even)*

- Can include social advantages which benefit family members of workers *(Cristini)*

  Nursery place falls within Article 7(2).

- Max has the same right to a nursery place for his son as German parents

  Under German law:

  Foreign nationals must be permanently resident in Germany.

  German nationals do not have to access to nursery.

This is a direct discrimination which cannot be justified.

2-) Educational grant

- Maintenance and training grant = 'social advantage' (Article 7(2) **Reg. 492/2011)** *(Lair)*

  Only a worker can claim

Worker =

- continuing employment relationship

or

- relationship between the purpose of the studies and previous employment

or

- became involuntarily unemployed and obliged by market conditions to undertake occupational retraining in another field of activity

Nothing to suggest Chris satisfies any of these. However, Article 10 of Regulation 492/2011 states that

- Equal access of migrant worker's children to State's general educational, apprenticeship and vocational training courses

Encompasses:

- not only rules relating to admission
- but also, general measures intended to facilitate
- educational attendance
- includes grants
- Article 10 extends to all forms of education

Reserving grants only to German nationals = direct discrimination. Chris is entitled to equal access to grant.

Alternative right to education grant as a Union citizen?

Articles 20(2) and 21 of the TFEU:

Right of Union citizens to move and reside freely.

These articles should be read with Article 18 TFEU.

Prohibits discrimination on grounds of nationality.

This can extend to education grants *(Bidar)* (See also Article 24 of Directive 2004/38)

However, Union citizen rights are subject to the conditions and limitations in the Treaties and secondary measures. (See Articles 20(2) & 21 TFEU; also see Article 24(1) of Directive 2004/38).

Chris has a right under Article 10 of Regulation 492/2011.

Important Case list:

Education Rights

R (Bidar) v Ealing LBC (Case C-209/03) [2005] ECR I-2119

Blaizot v University of Liége (Case 24/86) [1988] ECR 379

Brown v Secretary of State for Scotland (Case 197/86) [1988] ECR 3205

Graiver v City of Liége (Case 293/83) [1985] ECR 593

Lair v Universität Hannover (Case 39/86) [1988] ECR 3161

Employment Rights

Angonese v Cassa di Risparmio di Bolzano S.p.A. (Case 281/98) [2000] ECR 1-4139

Gül v Regierungspräsident Düsseldorf (Case 131/85) [1986] ECR 1573

Sotqiu v Deutsche Bundespost (Case 152/73) [1974] ECR 153

Discrimination

Anita Groener v Minister for Education and City of Dublin Vocational Education Committee (Case 379/87) [1990] 1 CMLR 401

Commission v France (Case 167/73) [1974] ECR 359

Social Advantages/Rights

Cowan v Tresor Public (Case 186/87) [1989] ECR 195

Cristini v S.N.C.F. (Case 32/75) [1975] ECR 1085

Ministére Public v Even (Case 207/78) [1979] ECR 2019

CHAPTER VIII

FREEDOM OF ESTABLISHMENT

Learning Outcomes:

In this chapter, you should be able to understand:

- ✓ when article 49 of the TFEU is applicable;
- ✓ the prohibition on restrictions;
- ✓ how a restriction can be lawfully justified;
- ✓ how article 49 of the TFEU applies to companies/self-employed persons.

Questions and Answers:

1. **When is Article 49 of the TFEU applicable?**

Article 49 states that

> "Within the framework of the provisions set out below, restrictions on the freedom of establishment of nationals of a Member State in the territory of another Member State shall be prohibited. Such prohibition shall also apply to restrictions on the setting-up of agencies, branches or subsidiaries by nationals of any Member State established in the territory of any Member State.

> Freedom of establishment shall include the right to take up and pursue activities as self-employed persons and to set up and manage undertakings, in particular companies or firms within the meaning of the second paragraph of Article 54 of the TFEU, under the conditions laid down for its own nationals by the law of the country where such establishment is effected, subject to the provisions of the Chapter relating to capital."

Paragraph one prohibits limitations on the freedom to set up companies and firms (See also Article 54). This prohibition in the first paragraph includes restrictions on secondary forms of establishment, such as agencies, branches and subsidiaries.

The second paragraph safeguards the right of individuals to undertake self-employed work on an equal basis with citizens of the host Member State.

2. What constitutes establishment?

Establishment requires a person, a firm or a company to have a **permanent presence** in a Member State for **economic reasons**. For instance, it may involve a company or person moving to another Member State permanently in order to carry on business there or to establish a permanent branch in another Member State *(Gebhard)*.

'Economic activities' particularly involve industrial activities, activities of a commercial nature, activities of craftspeople and of the professions *(Jany, para. 7)*.

3. What is company and firm?

Article 54 of the TFEU states that

> "Companies or firms formed in accordance with the law of a Member State and having their registered office, central administration or principal place of business within the Union shall, for the purposes of this Chapter, be treated in the same way as natural persons who are nationals of Member States.
>
> 'Companies or firms' means companies or firms constituted under civil or commercial law, including cooperative societies, and other legal persons governed by public or private law, save for those which are non-profit-making."

A company or firm which meets the conditions stipulated in Article 54 may take advantage of the right protected by Article 49 to establish agencies, branches or subsidiaries in another Member State.

4. Who is a self-employed?

The term self-employed refers to persons who are:

- ✓ not in a situation of subordination regarding the choice of that activity, working conditions and conditions of remuneration;
- ✓ responsibility for themselves; and
- ✓ receive remuneration paid directly and in full to that person *(Jany, para 70)*.

5. What matters fall outside Article 49 of the TFEU?

There are two matters:

✓ The exercise of official authority:

Article 51 of the TFEU states that

> "The provisions of this Chapter shall not apply, so far as any given Member State is concerned, to activities which in that State are connected, even occasionally, with the exercise of official authority. The European Parliament and the Council, acting in accordance with the ordinary legislative procedure, may rule that the provisions of this Chapter shall not apply to certain activities."

The concept of official authority was explained in the case of **Reyners**:

> "Official authority is that which arises from the sovereignty and majesty of the state; for them who exercise it, it implies the power of enjoying the prerogatives outside the general law, privileges of official power and powers of coercion over citizens."

In this case, the Court of Justice also stated that the official authority exception "constitute[s] a **direct and specific connexion** with the exercise of official authority" (para. 45) **(Bold added)**.

✓ Internal situations:

As the first sentence of Article 49 of the TFEU mentions Member State nationals wishing to set themselves up in another Member State, the question is as to whether Article 49 can be applied domestically. An instance where the application of Article 49 against the home state arises is when a national of a Member State wishes to return to his home country to work as a self-employed person with less stringent qualifications obtained in another Member State. In sum, Article 49 does not apply in purely internal situations, but it is applicable if there is a cross border element **(Auer)**.

In the case of **Knoors**, the applicant was a Dutch citizen who received training as an engine fitter in his home country, but later moved to Belgium. In 1976 he made an application to work as a plumber in the Netherlands, but his application was rejected on the basis that he did not have the required Dutch qualifications. The Court of Justice held that

> "Although it is true that the provisions of the Treaty relating to establishment and the provision of services cannot be applied to situations which are purely internal to a Member State, the position nevertheless remains that the reference in Article 52 to "nationals of a Member State" who wish to establish themselves "in the territory of another Member State" cannot be interpreted in such a way as to exclude from the benefit of Community law a given Member State's

own nationals when the latter, owing to the fact that they have lawfully resided on the territory of another Member State and have there acquired a trade qualification which is recognized by the provisions of Community law, are, with regard to their State of origin, in a situation which may be assimilated to that of any other persons enjoying the rights and liberties guaranteed by the Treaty" (para. 24).

6. **What constitutes a restriction under Article 49 of the TFEU?**

Provisions that directly discriminate on the criteria of nationality constitute a clear breach of Article 49. It should be noted that any national measures must prohibit, impede or make less attractive the freedom of establishment *(CaixaBank France)*.

Furthermore, Article 49 incorporates other indirect types of discrimination and potentially other indistinctly applicable limitations (indirect discrimination) *(Ordre des Avocats v Klopp)*.

7. **How to justify restrictions?**

There are two options to justify restrictions:

✓ **The derogations**:

Article 52 TFEU states that

"1. The provisions of this Chapter and measures taken in pursuance thereof shall not prejudice the applicability of provisions laid down by law, regulation or administrative action providing for special treatment for foreign nationals on grounds of public policy, public security or public health.

2. The European Parliament and the Council shall, acting in accordance with the ordinary legislative procedure, issue directives for the coordination of the abovementioned provisions."

It should be noted that all derogations must be proportionate. It might be applied in direct discrimination as well as in indirect discrimination situations.

✓ **Imperative requirements**:

Restrictions which do not discriminate directly may be argued for on the grounds of imperative requirements in the interests of the public. These grounds have been set down by the Court of Justice. In the case of *Gebhard*, the Court of Justice found that if national measures which may hinder or make less attractive citizens' enjoyment of the freedom of establishment, the following conditions have to be satisfied for justification:

- **They must be applied in a non-discriminatory manner (indirect discrimination);**
- **They must be justified by imperative requirements in the general interest;**
- **They must be suitable for securing the attainment of the objective which they pursue; and;**
- **They must not go beyond what is necessary in order to attain it.**

8. **What about Professional Qualifications under Article 53 of the TFEU?**

Article 53 states that

> "1. In order to make it easier for persons to take up and pursue activities as self-employed persons, the European Parliament and the Council shall, acting in accordance with the ordinary legislative procedure, issue directives for the mutual recognition of diplomas, certificates and other evidence of formal qualifications and for the coordination of the provisions laid down by law, regulation or administrative action in Member States concerning the taking-up and pursuit of activities as self-employed persons.
>
> 2. In the case of the medical and allied and pharmaceutical professions, the progressive abolition of restrictions shall be dependent upon coordination of the conditions for their exercise in the various Member States."

The important point in this Article is that 'the mutual recognition of qualifications'. In the case of ***Thieffry***, the Court held that

> "The only purpose of mutual recognition of diplomas is to remove the obstacle deriving from the legitimate concern of a Member State to restrict access to certain professions to persons giving proof of specific professional qualifications, confirmed by diploma, by means of assuring that Member State that the professional qualifications acquired in another Member State are equivalent..." (p. 772).

The mutual recognition is only applicable in the case of EU qualifications. Members states are also able to introduce similar provisions with non-EU states as long as they are on an individual basis ***(Tawil-Albertini)***.

CASE STUDY:

1-) Alex is the proprietor and managing director of an IT company called GDL Ltd, which was founded in Germany and has its head office in Berlin. The company functions as a consultancy that assists the implementation of major computer projects in the public and private sectors.

Alex is seeking opportunities for GDL Ltd to obtain contracts in Romania, which he believes is a country with good prospects for his company. He thinks it would be an advantage for GDL Ltd to have an office in Romania, as this would help it to make successful bids for contracts. Furthermore, it would give the company a foothold in the country from where it could grow. However, Alex has been made aware of new Romanian legislation that introduces a condition whereby any IT company establishing an office in Romania must have a minimum level of paid up share capital that is at least as much as that of Romanian IT companies. The present minimum for Romanian IT companies is €100,000. This condition is designed to ensure that in the event of a company going bankrupt, creditors' claims would be met. This contrasts with German Law, which demands a much lower level of share capital for companies incorporated in Germany.

Give advice to GDL Ltd on the EU law on freedom of establishment.

Issue:

GDL Ltd — Minimum share capital requirement in Romania

Application:

Article 49: Establishment must have

Permanent basis or without foreseeable limit to its duration

Participation on a stable and continuous basis

GDL Ltd wants to set up a permanent office in Romania. So, it is an establishment.

Article 49 prohibits freedom of establishment restrictions on nationals of a Member State.

- **Can a 'national' include a company?**

  Yes, Article 54 must:

  − Be formed in accordance with law of a Member State

- Have its

    registered office

    central administration or

    principal place of business etc

  within the EU

- Be profit making

Article 49 applicable to GDL Plc.

- **Does freedom of establishment include establishment of an office?**

  Yes, it applies to setting-up agencies, branches or subsidiaries by nationals of any Member State (Article 49).

Limitations

1) Official authority exemption (Article 51)

- Must have direct and specific connection to official authority *(Reyners)*
  Test is not satisfied here.

2) Purely internal situations (Article 49)

- Nationals in the territory of another Member State
  GDL Ltd in Germany.
  Wishes to establish office in Romania
  Clearly not an internal situation.

Is the requirement a restriction on freedom of establishment?

- **What is a restriction?**
  (CaixaBank France)

  All measures which prohibit, impede or render less attractive the exercise of that freedom

- **Is the minimum share capital requirement a restriction?**

  Yes *(CaixaBank France test)*

Justifying the restriction

1) By derogation

- Article 52(1):
  public policy;

public security or
public health.

– **Proportionate?**
None of the above-mentioned grounds applicable.

2) By imperative requirements

– *(Gebhard)*
Non-discriminatory application;
Imperative requirement;
Suitable for the objective and;
Not go beyond what is necessary;
No imperative requirements.

In conclusion, there is a violation of Article 49.

2-) Ali is a citizen of France. He attended university in Turkey, gaining a Master's degree in architecture. He subsequently trained and qualified as an architect in Turkey. He then moved to Germany and, after gaining permission to practice his profession, worked for several years there for a company of architects. He set up his own business as an architect, and has run it in Germany for six years. After being divorced from his wife, he has decided to return to France and move his company there. But the French authorities have informed him that he cannot register as an architect unless he has a qualification recognised by French law. Hence, Ali cannot work as an architect in France without being registered there.

Instruct Ali concerning the EU law on freedom of establishment.

Issue:

Refusal to recognise Ali's qualification and experience

Application:

• **Self-employed (Article 49) or worker (Article 45)?**

Test for self-employed *(Jany)*:
Acts outside of any relationship of subordination
Under the person's own responsibility
In return for remuneration

Contrast test for worker under *Lawrie-Blum*

Running his own business
Ali is a self-employed.

- **Establishment?**

Yes, because he has a permanent basis.

- **Can Article 49 be relied upon by Ali against his own Member State?**

Applies to nationals of a Member State in the territory of another member state *(Knoors)*

  – Does not apply to purely internal situations within a Member State
  – But a degree of externality may suffice

Article 49 can be relied upon by Ali against France.

- **Qualification from EU**

  – Subsequent shift to mutual recognition approach.
  – Ali is a French citizen, but his qualification from Turkey. But he was authorised to practice as an architect in Germany.

- **Qualification from outside EU**

The mutual recognition principle is not applicable in this case.

If Ali was authorized to practice in Germany, he is also allowed to practice in France.

Important Case list:

Companies and Firms

Centros Ltd v Erhvervs-og Selskabsstryrelsen (Case C-212/97) [1999] 2 CMLR 551

Concept of Establishment

Caixa Bank France v Ministére de L'Economie (Case C-442/02) [2004] ECR I-8961.

Reinhard Gebhard v Consiglio Dell'Ordine degli Avvocati E Procuratori di Milano (Case 55/94)[1996] 1 CMLR 603

Jany v Staastssecretaris van Justitite (Case C-268/99) [2001] ECR I-8615

Jean Reyners v The Belgian State (Case 2/74) [1974] 2 CMLR 305

Thieffry v Conseil de l'Ordre des Avocats a la Cour de Paris (Paris Bas Council) (Case 71/76) [1977] 2 CMLR 373

Internal Situations

J. Knoors v Secretary of State for Economic Affairs (Case 115/78) [1979] 2 CMLR 357

Ministére Public v Vincent Auer (Case 136/78) [1979] 2 CMLR 373

Recognition of Qualification

Abdullah Tawil-Albertini v Ministre des Affaires Sociales (Case C-154/93) [1995] 1 CMLR 612

Irene Vlasspoulou v Ministerium für Justiz, Bundes- und Europaangelegenheiten Baden-

Salomone Haim v Kassenzahnärztliche Vereinigung Nordrhein (Case C-319/92) [1994] 2 CMLR 169 (Haim I)

Würremberg (Ministry of Justice, Federal and European Affairs of the Province of Baden-

Württemberg) (Case 340/89) [1993] 2 CMLR 221

Restrictions

Ordre des Avocats Au Barreau de Paris (Paris Bar Council) v Rechtsanwalt Onno Klopp

(Case 107/83) [1985] 1 CMLR 99

CHAPTER IX

FREEDOM TO PROVIDE SERVICES

Learning Outcomes:

In this chapter, you should be able to understand:

- ✓ when article 56 of the TFEU is applicable;
- ✓ the prohibition on restrictions;
- ✓ how a restriction can be lawfully justified;
- ✓ how article 56 of the TFEU applies to companies/self-employed persons.

Questions and Answers:

1. **When is Article 56 of the TFEU applicable?**

   Article 56 states that

   "Within the framework of the provisions set out below, restrictions on freedom to provide services within the Union shall be prohibited in respect of nationals of Member States who are established in a Member State other than that of the person for whom the services are intended.

   The European Parliament and the Council, acting in accordance with the ordinary legislative procedure, may extend the provisions of the Chapter to nationals of a third country who provide services and who are established within the Union."

   Article 56 also covers self-employed people.

2. **What constitutes a service?**

   Article 57 of the TFEU states that

   "Services shall be considered to be 'services' within the meaning of the Treaties where they are normally provided for remuneration, in so far as they are not governed by the provisions relating to freedom of movement for goods, capital and persons.

   'Services' shall in particular include:

(a) activities of an industrial character;

(b) activities of a commercial character;

(c) activities of craftsmen;

(d) activities of the professions.

Without prejudice to the provisions of the Chapter relating to the right of establishment, the person providing a service may, in order to do so, temporarily pursue his activity in the Member State where the service is provided, under the same conditions as are imposed by that State on its own nationals."

Please note that this list is not exhaustive. This list can be extended by the Court of Justice. For instance, medical termination of a pregnancy performed for remuneration constituted a service *(Grogan)*. In addition, sport is also a service *(Deliège)*.

In order to qualify as a service, the activity in question must meet the following conditions *(Steymann)*:

a-) The remuneration does not have to be paid by the person in receipt of the service, but can be paid by a third party;

b-) The service in question must be a genuine and effective economic activity, not marginal or secondary;

c-) The service must be of a temporary nature in the Member States.

3. **What matters falling outside Article 56 of the TFEU?**

There are three matters:

✓ **The exercise of official authority:**

Article 62 of the TFEU states that the exception in Article 51 of the TFEU pertaining to official authority also applies to the freedom to provide services under Article 56 of the TFEU.

✓ **Internal situations:**

Article 56 of the TFEU prohibits restrictions on the freedom to provide services only "in respect of nationals of Members States who are established in a Member State other than that of the person for whom the services are intended." It follows that Article 56 does not apply to purely internal situations unless there is a cross border element.

✓ **Where provisions for other areas such as Goods, Capital or Persons govern:**

Article 57(1) of the TFEU states that

> "Services shall be considered to be 'services' within the meaning of the Treaties where they are normally provided for remuneration, in so far as they are not governed by the provisions relating to freedom of movement for goods, capital and persons."

In the case of ***Omega***, the Court of Justice concluded that Article 56 of the TFEU will apply where other applicable freedoms are secondary to the freedom to provide services.

4. **What constitutes a restriction under Articles 56 and 57 of the TFEU?**

Article 56(1) states that

> "…restrictions on freedom to provide services within the Union shall be prohibited in respect of nationals of Member States who are established in a Member State other than that of the person for whom the services are intended."

Article 57 also adds that

> "…the person providing a service may, in order to do so, temporarily pursue his activity in the Member State where the service is provided, under the same conditions as are imposed by that State on its own nationals."

Article 56 and 57 prohibits measures which discriminate against service providers not only on the basis of nationality but also on the basis of residence *(**van Binsbergen**)*.

5. **How to justify restrictions?**

There are two options to justify restrictions:

✓ **The derogations:**

Article 62 of the TFEU extends the derogations listed in Article 52 of the TFEU to services.

It should be noted that all derogations must be proportionate. It might be applied in direct discrimination as well as in indirect discrimination situations.

✓ **Imperative reasons:**

Restrictions that do not discriminate in a direct way can also be based on imperative reasons. They are established by the Court of Justice. The same following conditions, stated in the case of ***Gebhard***, must be satisfied:

- They must be applied in a non-discriminatory manner (indirect discrimination);
- They must be justified by imperative requirements in the general interest;
- They must be suitable for securing the attainment of the objective which they pursue; and
- They must not go beyond what is necessary in order to attain it.

The Court of Justice gave the following examples as imperative reasons in the cases of ***Gouda and Kohll***:

- Professional rules intended to protect recipients of the service;
- Protection of intellectual property;
- The protection of workers;
- Consumer protection;
- The conservation of the national historic and artistic heritage;
- Dissemination of knowledge of the artistic and cultural heritage of a country;
- Possible risk of seriously undermining social security system's financial balance.

6. **What rights are granted by the freedom to provide services?**

   ✓ The right to move in another Member State to provide services.
   ✓ The right to reside in another Member State to provide services.
   ✓ The right to operate as a business in another Member State.

7. **What about professional qualifications under Article 53 of the TFEU?**

   Article 53 is also applicable in conjunction with Article 56 of the TFEU. In addition, Title II of Directive 2005/36 is now the main criteria as regards the recognition of professional qualifications concerning the freedom to provide services. This applies when two main conditions are met. Firstly, as noted in Section 8.9.1, Directive 2005/36 only governs nationals of a Member State seeking to carry on a regulated profession outside their home Member State (Article 2). Secondly, Title II is only applicable when a person who already provides services legally in another Member State returns to the host Member State temporarily and on a random basis to carry on the same profession (Article 5). It is not applicable in the event of the services in question being provided in the host Member State while the service provider has not moved there *(X-Steurberatungsgesellschaft)*.

Please also note that the mutual recognition is also applicable in the case of EU qualifications. Member states are able to make similar agreements with non-EU states on a solely individual basis.

CASE STUDY:

1-) Alex is the proprietor and managing director of an IT company called GDL Ltd, which was founded in Germany and has its head office in Berlin. The company functions as a consultancy that assists the implementation of major computer projects in the public and private sectors.

Alex is aware that the public sector in Romania is undergoing restructuring and believes his company could obtain contracts in this area, although it does not have an office there. However, Romanian law stipulates that all IT projects in the government sector must be carried out by Romanian companies on account of national security issues.

Give advice to GDL Ltd concerning the EU law on the Freedom to Provide Services.

Issue:

Nationality requirement for Government IT projects

Application:

Services (Article 56)

Temporarily pursued in Member State (Article 57) or no presence there

Determined on basis of:

- Duration of service; and
- Regularity, periodicity or continuity *(Gebhard)*

No permanent presence in Romania.

IT projects: Are they services?

Genuine and effective economic activity?

Yes

Provided for remuneration?

Yes

Article 56 prohibits FPS restrictions on nationals of a Member State.
- **Can a 'national' include a company?**
  Yes, Article 62 applies Article 54 which must:

  Be formed in accordance with law of a Member State

  – Have its

  registered office

  central administration or

  principal place of business etc

  within the EU

  – Be profit making

  Article 56 is applicable in this case.

Limitations

  ✓ **Official authority exemption (Article 51)**
  – Where connected, even occasionally, with the exercise of official authority
  – Must have direct and specific connection to official authority *(Reyners)*

  Sufficient connection here?

  No

  ✓ **Purely internal situations**
  Article 56: Prohibits restrictions for nationals established in a Member State other than that of the person for whom the services are intended.

  – GDL Plc established in Germany

– Wishes to provide services in Romania
– **Clearly not an internal situation here**

Article 57: Must not be governed by provisions for goods, capital and persons

No, any effect on goods (IT parts) is secondary to restriction on services *(Omega)*.

What constitutes a restriction?

Restriction = liable to prohibit or impede a provider in another Member State.

Also, where liable to render less attractive

• **Is nationality requirement a restriction?**
Yes, prohibits foreign companies providing service.

Can nationality requirement be justified?

– **By imperative reasons?**
No, it is not indistinctly applicable.

– **By derogation?**
Which potential ground?
May be public security.

– **Proportionate?**
No, because it applies to all projects even where national security not involved.

2-) GDL Ltd has set up an office in Romania but has encountered problems with its accounting systems. It wants Michael, who is a French national, to deal with these problems. Michael is qualified as a chartered accountant in France and has worked for GDL Ltd before. He is considered to be one of the best in his field. He would offer his services on a self-employed basis for as long as is necessary to resolve the problems. However, the Romanian authorities have told Michael he is not permitted to practise in Romania since national law requires anyone working as a chartered accountant in Romania to have the necessary Romanian qualification. This can only be obtained by attending a degree-level accountancy course at a Romanian University and completing a two-year period of training. Despite this, Alex still wants GDL Ltd to employ Michael.

Give advice to Michael relating to the EU law on the Freedom to Provide Services.

Issue:

Prohibition on Michael practising as a Chartered Accountant

Application:

- **Services?**
  Yes

  Temporarily pursuing activity (Article 57)

  Services include "activities of the professions" (Article 57(d))

- **Self-employed?**
  Jany:
  Acts outside of any relationship of subordination
  Under the person's own responsibility
  In return for remuneration

  Acting as independent contractor, so **Michael is a self-employed.**

- **Development**
  Initially direct discrimination *(Reyners)*
  Subsequent shift to mutual recognition approach in *(Thieffry)*

  Same principles apply where providing services under Article 56.

In conclusion, application to Michael:

He is a top trouble-shooter in this area.

It is very likely sufficient qualifications and knowledge.

Important Case list:

Christelle Deliége v Ligue Francophone de Judo et Disciplines Associees ASBL and Others (Joined Cases 51/96 and 191/97) [2002] 2 CMLR 65

Graziana Luisi and Giuseppe Carbone v Ministero del Tesoro (Cases 286/82 & 26/83) [1985] 3 CMLR 52

Procureur du Roi v Marc Debauve and Others (Case 52/79) [1981] 2 CMLR 362

Raymond Kohll v Union des caisses de maladie (Case C-158/96) [1998] 1998 I-01931

Reinhard Gebhard v Consiglio Dell'Ordine degli Avvocati E Procuratori di Milano (Case 55/94) [1996] 1 CMLR 603

Society for the Protection of Unborn Children Ireland Ltd. (S.P.U.C.) v Stephen Grogan and Others (Case C-159/90) [1991] 3 CMLR 849

Stichting Collectieve Antennevoorziening Gouda and others v Commissariaat voor de Media (Case C-288/89) [1991] 1991 I-04007

Omega Spielhallen- und Automatenaufstellungs-GmbH v Oberbürger-meisterin der Bundesstadt Bonn (Case C-36/02) [2004] ECR I-9609

X-Steurberatungsgesellschaft v Finanzamt Hannover-Nord (Case C-342/14) [2015] ECR I-0000

Van Binsbergen v Nesturr van de Bedrifsvereniging voor de Metaalnverheid (Case 33/74) [1974] ECR 1299

CHAPTER X

COMPETITION LAW: COLLUSION AND ABUSE OF DOMINANCE

Learning Outcomes:

In this chapter, you should be able to understand:

- ✓ the forms of collusion prohibited by Article101(1) of the TFEU;
- ✓ the exemptions provided by Article 101(3) of the TFEU and Regulation 330/2010;
- ✓ the law on Article 102 of the TFEU related to abuse of dominance;
- ✓ the requirements for abuse of dominance.

Questions and Answers:

1. **What is Article 101 of the TFEU about? What are key elements under Article 101(1) of the TFEU?**

   There are three paragraphs in Article 101:

   - ✓ First paragraph prohibits anti-competitive collusion
   - ✓ Second paragraph states that any agreements or decisions prohibited pursuant to this Article shall be automatically void.
   - ✓ Third paragraph deals with exemptions.

   Please also note that three main elements in Article 101(1):

   a-) all agreements between undertakings, decisions by associations of undertakings and concerted practices

   b-) which may affect trade between Member States and

   c-) which have as their object or effect the prevention, restriction or distortion of competition within the internal market.

2. **What are agreements; undertakings; associations of undertakings and concerted practices?**

   Agreements has been interpreted broadly including formal written, oral agreements, gentleman agreements etc.

Undertakings means that "…the concept of an undertaking encompasses every entity engaged in an economic activity, regardless of the legal status of the entity and the way in which it is financed and, secondly, that employment procurement is an economic activity' *(Höfner and Else, para. 21)*.

Associations of undertakings include trade associations, co-operatives and lawyer chambers and so on.

Concerted practice means that "A form of co-ordination between undertakings which, without having reached the stage where an agreement properly so-called has been concluded, knowingly substitutes practical co-operation between them for the risks of competition" *(Dyestuffs, para. 64)*.

3. **What does 'effect on trade between Member States' mean?**

In the case of the *S.T.M.*, the Court of Justice stated that:

"…It must be possible to foresee with a sufficient degree of probability on the basis of a set of objective factors of law or of fact that the agreement in question may have an influence, direct or indirect, actual or potential, on the pattern of trade between Member States" (p.249).

4. **What does 'object or effect the prevention, restriction or distortion of competition within the internal market' mean?**

Article 101(1) bans agreements which aim to prevent, restrict or distort competition within the internal market. A non-exhaustive list of prohibited restrictions is given. It is referred to as a 'black list'.

The aim of an agreement is ascertained by examining the objective of an agreement in the economic circumstances under which the agreement will function *(S.T.M.)*.

If the aim of an agreement does not involve restricting competition, evidence must be provided to the effect that the agreement would, in practice, result in restricting competition. In order for this to happen, an agreement must be analysed fully, as must the market affected *(European Night Services)*.

5. **What is the blacklist under Article 101(1) of the TFEU?**

(a) directly or indirectly fix purchase or selling prices or any other trading conditions;

(b) limit or control production, markets, technical development, or investment;

(c) share markets or sources of supply;

(d) apply dissimilar conditions to equivalent transactions with other trading parties, thereby placing them at a competitive disadvantage;

(e) make the conclusion of contracts subject to acceptance by the other parties of supplementary obligations which, by their nature or according to commercial usage, have no connection with the subject of such contracts.

6. What are the defense mechanisms?

There are two defense mechanisms that may be used to justify the competition:

✓ **Rule of reason approach**: If the pro-competitive effects are greater than its anti-competitive effects, the Court may rule that Article 101 has not been breached on account of the overall effect not preventing, restricting or distorting competition *(S.T.M.)*.

✓ **The De Minimis defense**: An agreement is not banned by Article 101(1) if its effect on competition or trade between states is not 'appreciable'. The effect will be considered to be too *De Minimis*. This defense mechanism may only be used when the consequences of the agreement prevent, restrict or distort competition *(Vök)*.

The European Commission, in its Notice on Agreements of Minor Importance (2014) OJ C291/01, usually referred to as the *De Minimis* Notice, stated that horizontal agreements between undertakings with an aggregate market share not more than 10% do not appreciably impinge on competition within the meaning of Article 101(1). As for vertical agreements, they do not appreciably affect competition when the market share of undertaking is not more than 15%.

It is important to note that horizontal agreements are made between undertakings at the same level of trade or industry. For example, A and B are two undertakings that are suppliers. Vertical agreements are made between undertakings functioning on different levels. For example, A is a supplier and B is a manufacturer.

7. What are exemptions?

Two types of exemption exist: Individual and block.

✓ **Individual exemptions**: Article 101(3) makes clear that the provisions contained in Article 101(1) cannot be applied in connection with agreements, decisions and concerted practices, or with types of agreement, decisions and concerted practices that meet the four conditions (two positive and two negative) in Article 101(3):

- **Positive: an agreement, decision or concerted practice must**

  1-) contribute to improving the production or distribution of goods or to promoting technical or economic progress; and

  2-) Provide consumers with a fair share of the resulting benefit. The term 'resulting benefit' includes product improvement, technical or economic progress, benefits to consumer.

- **Negative: additionally, an agreement, decision or concerted practice must not**

  3-) impose on the undertakings concerned restrictions which are not indispensable to the attainment of these objectives; and

  4-) afford such undertakings the possibility of eliminating competition in respect of a substantial part of the products in question.

- ✓ **Block exemptions**: Block exemptions are mentioned in Article 101(3) with reference to 'categories of agreements'. Regulation 330/2010 is an example of a block exemption. In this Regulation, some vertical agreements are exempted (Article 2(1)). Vertical agreements are those made between undertakings functioning at different levels of the supply chain. An example would be an agreement between supplier and manufacturer. This exemption is conditional on the market share of the supplier being not more than 30% of the market in question (Article 3(1)).
  Please note that Regulation 1/2003 is also related to block exemptions.

8. **What are the key elements under Article 102 of the TFEU?**

Article 102 states that

> "Any **abuse** by one or more **undertakings** of a **dominant position** within the internal market or in a substantial part of it shall be prohibited as incompatible with the internal market in so far as it may **affect trade between Member States**" **(Bold added).**

There are four key elements:

- ✓ There must be one or more undertakings (See question 2 to understand the meaning of undertakings);
- ✓ In a dominant position within the internal market;
- ✓ Abuse of a dominant position;

✓ May affect trade between Member States (See question 3 to understand the meaning of this).

9. How to know whether there is a dominant position?

The Court of Justice in the case of ***United Brands*** defined the meaning of dominance as follows:

"The dominant position referred to in Article 82 EC relates to a position of economic strength enjoyed by an undertaking which enables it to prevent effective competition being maintained on the relevant market by giving it the power to behave to an appreciable extent independently of its competitors, customers and ultimately, of its consumers" (para. 65).

There are several factors to establish whether an undertaking has a dominant position:

✓ **Brand identification**: As time passes, consumers tend to associate a brand name with a product and will often be reluctant to try another product sold by a different company ***(United Brands)***.

✓ **Intellectual property rights**: In the case of ***Hugin***, the company was the sole manufacturer of spare parts of Hugin cash registers in the UK, as they had patented the design for the cash registers.

✓ **Market share**: What determines whether an undertaking has a dominant position is the relative share of the market that it possesses. E.g., ***United Brands*** has a dominant position in the market in bananas as they have a 40% to 45% share, while the closest competitor has only a 17% share.

✓ **Sophisticated distribution and sales networks**: In ***Michelin I***, this company has a sophisticated structure of commercial agents much larger than those of its competitors. This allows it to directly reach dealers and tyre consumers at all times.

✓ **Superior technology**: In the case of ***Hoffmann-La Roche***, the company was ahead of its competitors technologically, not solely as regards the vitamins it produced, but also on account of the highly advanced technical service it had developed to advise and help its customers to use their products.

✓ **Vertical integration**: This term concerns having control over the entire process of taking a product into the market, all the way from production to distribution and to the eventual sale to consumers ***(United Brands)***.

✓ **Wealth of capital and financial barriers**: An example of this is when a rich company takes advantage of its financial advantage to stifle competition by utilising predatory pricing policies ***(AKZO)***.

10. What is relevant market?

To ascertain that an undertaking's actions have contravened Article 102, the Commission needs to establish the market in which the undertaking is active. The European Commission stated the definition of relevant market in its Notice on the Definition of Relevant Market for the Purposes of Community Law (97/C 372/03) (1997) OJ C372/5:

> "Market definition is a tool to identify and define the boundaries of competition between firms. It serves to establish the framework within which competition policy is applied by the Commission. The main purpose of market definition is to identify in a systematic way the competitive constraints that the undertakings involved (2) face. The objective of defining a market in both its product and geographic dimension is to identify those actual competitors of the undertakings involved that are capable of constraining those undertakings' behaviour and of preventing them from behaving independently of effective competitive pressure. It is from this perspective that the market definition makes it possible inter alia to calculate market shares that would convey meaningful information regarding market power for the purposes of assessing dominance or for the purposes of applying Article 85." (para. 2)

To clearly define 'the relevant market', both the product and the geographic extent of the market need to be analysed.

Relevant product market is defined as follows:

> "A relevant product market comprises all those products and/or services which are regarded as interchangeable or substitutable by the consumer, by reason of the products' characteristics, their prices and their intended use" (para. 7).

Relevant geographic market is defined as follows:

> "The relevant geographic market comprises the area in which the undertakings concerned are involved in the supply and Remand of products or services, in which the conditions of competition are sufficiently homogeneous and which can be distinguished from neighbouring areas because the conditions of competition are appreciably different in those area" (para. 8).

In addition, it would be necessary to check the relevant market's time dimensions.

11. What is an abuse of dominant position? Any example?

Commanding a dominant position in a market does not constitute, by itself, a breach of Article 102. There must be an abuse of that dominant position. Such abuse may, in particular, consist in:

(a) directly or indirectly imposing unfair purchase or selling prices or other unfair trading conditions;

(b) limiting production, markets or technical development to the prejudice of consumers;

(c) applying dissimilar conditions to equivalent transactions with other trading parties, thereby placing them at a competitive disadvantage;

(d) making the conclusion of contracts subject to acceptance by the other parties of supplementary obligations which, by their nature or according to commercial usage, have no connection with the subject of such contracts.

CASE STUDY:

The Computer World is a company based in Germany. It specialises in the manufacture of computers. In June 2010, it brought out a new product, a tablet device called the 'Magic'.

Thanks to its modern features and durable batteries, 'Magic' turned out to be very popular. In order to continue its growth, the Computer World began negotiations with one of their Belgian distributors, Tablet SA. Tablet SA had owned exclusive distribution rights for the Computer World products in Belgium since 1987.

The Computer World was confident that the 'Magic' would sell well in Belgium and it wished to add new clauses to its existing distribution agreement with Tablet SA. The proposed terms included:

a-) Tablet SA will not offer the 'Magic' for sale in Germany;

b-) Tablet SA will not be permitted to put the 'Magic' on their website for sale to customers resident in Germany;

c-) Tablet SA will sell all 'Magic'. Supplies will come solely from the Computer World;

d-) Tablet SA will not sell the 'Magic' for a price of less than 500 Euros.

Tablet SA accepted all these terms and in March 2012, the 'Magic' went on sale in Belgium.

As expected, the product sold well in Belgium, and by May 2014, the Computer World had gained 45% of the tablet market there. However, Tablet SA had carried out market research showing that consumers considered the 'Magic' produced by the Computer World to be limited in range and expensive. Consequently, Tablet SA informed the Computer World that it had entered an agreement with Oak SA, a Spanish company, in line with which Oak SA will supply Tablet SA with a broader and improved range of tablet. In response, the Computer World has threatened to take legal action against both Tablet SA and Oak SA. It has also threatened to halt their supply of the 'Magic' to Tablet SA and to use a different company for distribution, Ordinateur Monde SA.

Give advice to Tablet SA and Oak SA.

Issues:

✓ Collusion between the Computer World and Tablet SA under Article 101(1);

✓ Abuse of a dominant position of the Computer World under Article 102.

Application:

Common elements for Article 101(1) and Article 102:

Firstly, there must at least one undertaking. Tablet SA and Oak SA are a company engaged in economic activities. Therefore, they are an undertaking.

Secondly, there must be an agreement. There is a legally binding agreement between Tablet SA and the Computer World & Tablet SA and Oak SA.

Article 101(1): Collusion

1-) Is there a trade between Member States?

Yes, there is because of

Potential affect sufficient (***Société Technique Minière***)

Being used to exclude Spanish supplier

2-) What is an object or effect of agreement?

Does it prevent, restrict or distort competition?

(See Articles 101(1)(a)-(e))

Is it possible to use the defence mechanisms to justify?

- ## The *de minimis* principle

    - Vertical agreements in here between the Computer World and Pettit-Tel SA *(Völk)*:

    Market share of each of the parties

    Must not exceed <u>15%</u> share of any of the relevant markets

    - ## Application:
    ### What is the relevant market here?

    Tablet

    Market share for 'Universal' now 45% of tablet market

- ## The rule of reason

✓ Pro-competitive elements outweigh anti-competitive elements? *(Société Technique Minière)*

Consider:

✓ **Pro-Competitive**: This agreement enables 'Universal' to break into market

✓ **Anti-Competitive**: This agreement places restrictions on trade

In addition, block and individual exemptions should be checked:

- ## Block Exemptions

    Regulation 330/2010

✓ Block exemption for vertical agreements (Article 2). There is a vertical agreement in here.

✓ unless exceptions apply

✓ No exemption now that market share exceeds 30%

✓ Hardcore restrictions:

✓ Term B prohibits passive selling into another territory (Article 4(b))

✓ Term D sets minimum sale prices (Article 4(a))

    No block exemption.

- ## Individual exemptions

    Any agreement which individually satisfies Article 101(3) must contribute:

    to improving the production or distribution of goods or

to promoting technical or economic progress

While allowing consumers a fair share of the resulting benefit **must NOT**

(a) Impose restrictions which are not indispensable to these objectives; or

(b) Afford the possibility of eliminating competition.

No individual exemption.
In conclusion, it is very likely to say that Article 101(1) was violated.

Article 102:

1-) Is the undertaking dominant in that market?

In order to answer this question, it would be good to identify the relevant market firstly. Indeed, ***United Brand*** case states that position of economic strength preventing effective competition in **the relevant market.**

2-) What is the relevant market in this case?

Relevant market is an objective of defining market = to identify actual competitors by taking into account the following three dimensions:

✓ **Relevant Product Market ('RPM'):** products and/or services are interchangeable or substitutable
   Tablet
✓ **Relevant Geographical Market ('RGM'):**
   undertakings are involved in supply and demand of products or services;
   conditions of competition are sufficiently homogeneous;
   and are appreciably different from neighbouring areas.
   Belgium
✓ **Relevant Temporal Market ('RTM'):**
   Relevant period = From March 2010 to present

3-) Does the Computer World have a dominant position?

Market share: As of May 2014, it was 45%.

Brand: In light of the market share, it also seems that they have an established name.

The Computer World has a dominant position. Please note that having a dominant position in a market does not, in itself, amount to a breach of Article 102.

4-) Is the Computer World abusing its dominant position?

The Computer World threatened to withdraw their supply of the 'Magic' to Tablet SA and to distribute through a different company.

5-) May abusing dominant position affect trade between member states?

- The affect:
    - Must be on trade between Member States
    - Can be potential.
- **Application:**

    - Threating Tablet SA out of business;

    - Preventing Spanish supplier entering the market.

Abusing dominant position may affect trade between member states.

In conclusion, it is a violation of Article 102.

Important Case List:

Abuse of Dominant Position

AKZO Chemie BV v Commission (Case C-62/86) [1991] ECR I-3359

Benzine en Petroleum Handelsmaatschappij BV v Commission (Case 77/77) [1978] ECR 1513 (ABG Oil)

Europemballage Corporation and Continental Can Company Inc. v Commission (Case 6/72) [1973] 1 CMLR 199

Hoffman-La-Roche & Co v Commission (Case 85/76) [1979] 3 CMLR 211

Hugin Kassaregister AB and Hugin Cash Registers Ltd v Commission Case 22/78 [1979] ECR 1869

Merci Concenzionali Porto di Genova SpA v Siderurgica Gabrielli SpA (Case C-179/90) [1991] ECR I-5889

Misrosoft v Commission (Case T-201/04) [2005] 4 CMLR 5

Nederlandsche Banden – Industrie Michelin NV v Commission (Case 322/81) [1985] 1 CMLR 282

Sealink/B & I Holyhead: Interim Measures (Sealink I) [1992] 5 CMLR 255

United Brands Company and United Brands Continental BV v Commission (Case 27/76) [1978] 1 CMLR 429

Collusion

Ahlström Osakeyhtiö and others v Commission (Cases 89, 104, 116-117 & 125-129/85) [1988] 4 CMLR 901 (the Wood Pulp Cartel)

Commission v ANIC Partecipazioni SpA (Case 49/92P) [2001] 4 CMLR 17

European Night Services and others v Commission (Cases T-374, 375, 384, 388/94) [1998] 5 CMLR 718

Höfner & Else v Macrotron GmbH (Case C-41-90) [1991] ECR-I-1979

Imperial Chemical Industries Ltd. v Commission (Case 48/69) [1972] CMLR 557 (Dyestuffs)

Métropole Télévision (M6) and others v Commission (Case T-112/99) [2001] ECR 11-02459

Pronuptia de Paris GmbH v Pronuptia de Paris Irmgard Schillgallis (Case 161/84) [1986] 1 CMLR 414

Société Technique Miniére v Maschinenbau Ulm GmbH (Case 32/65) [1966] CMLR 257 (the S.T.M.)

Völk v S.P.R.L. Etablissements J. Vervaecke (Case 5/69) [1969] CMLR 273

SUMMARY: SAMPLE TEST QUESTIONS

Direct Applicability/Direct Effect/Indirect Effect/State Liability

1) Of the definitions below, which is the best description of the principle 'direct applicability'?

a) An EU measure is one that affects everyone in the EU sine die.

b) Such a measure is deemed to be a kind of secondary legislation.

c) A measure of this type confers rights on citizens that are enforceable in national courts.

d) The measure in question automatically becomes part of national law.

2) Which one or more of the following sources of law are directly applicable?

a) Treaties

b) Regulations

c) Directives

d) Decisions

3) In which European case did the Court of Justice establish the principle of direct effect?

a) Van Gend en Loos v Nederlands

b) Van Duyn v Home Office

c) Costa v ENEL

d) Amministrazione delle Finanze dello Stato v Simmenthal SpA

4) Of these definitions, which most accurately expresses the principle of 'direct effect'?

a) That European law not only imposes obligations on individuals but grants them rights which are enforceable in their national court.

b) That European law places obligations on individuals and at the same time confers rights that may be implemented in the Court of Justice.

c) That national courts have to read national law in line with European law.

d) That the Court of Justice has an obligation to interpret national law in line with European law.

5) Which provisions may be directly effective?

a) Regulations only

b) Decisions only

c) Treaties, regulations, directives and decisions

d) Treaties and directives only

6) Which one or more of the following conditions is / are NOT pre-requisites for a regulation to have direct effect?

a) That the provision is unconditional.

b) That the time period for implementation has expired.

c) That the provision is sufficiently clear and precise.

d) That the regulation is being enforced against a state body.

7) Which case first established that directives were capable of having direct effect?

a) Defrenne v SABENA (No 2)

b) Van Duyn v Home Office

c) Marshall v Southampton and South West Area health Authority (Teaching) (No 1)

d) Dori (Faccini) v Recreb Sri

8) Which of the following conditions must be satisfied before a directive can be said to be directly effective?

That the provision is unconditional.

That the time period for implementation has expired.

That the provision is sufficiently clear and precise.

That the directive is being enforced against a state body.

a) 1, 2 & 3

b) 1, 3 & 4

c) 1, 2 & 4

d) All of the above

9) A directive can have vertical and horizontal effect?

a) True

b) False

10) Which of the following is/are NOT criteria to be satisfied before a body is deemed to be an 'emanation of the state'?

a) The body must be publicly funded.

b) The body must be under state control.

c) The body must have special powers.

d) The body must be providing a public service.

11) Which case established the criteria for establishing when a body is an emanation of the state?

a) Griffin v South West Water Services Ltd

b) Kampelmann v Landschaftsverband Westfalen-Lippe

c) Foster v British Gas plc

d) National Union of teachers v Governing Body of St Mary's Church of England School (Aided) Junior School

12) Which definition best describes the concept of 'indirect effect' which was established in the case of *Von Colson & Kamann v Land Nordhein-Westfalen*?

a) National courts must interpret national law in the light of the relevant directive.

b) National courts have an obligation to interpret European law in line with national law.

c) The Court of Justice has an obligation to interpret national law in accordance with the directive in question.

d) The Court of Justice has an obligation to interpret European law in line with the law of the Member State in question.

13) The principle of state liability is devised for what purpose?

a) To restore the circumstances of an individual to those that would have obtained in the event of a directive being put into effect.

b) To make good the losses suffered by an individual as a consequence of a Member state not meeting its obligations under European law.

c) To penalise the Member state in question.

d) To compel the Member State to amend its law.

14) Which case established the principle of state liability?

a) Brasserie du Pecheur SA v Germany

b) R v Secretary of State for transport ex p Factortame Ltd (No 3)

c) Francovich & Bonifaci v Italian Republic

d) Dillenkofer and others v Germany

15) In way or ways did the joined cases of Brasserie du Pecheur v Germany and R v Secretary of State for Transport ex parte Factortame and others extend the principle of state liability enunciated in Francovich & Bonifaci v Italian Republic? (More than one option may be selected)

a) They extended the principle to cover any breach of EU Law.

b) They extended the principle to apply only to a breach of a Treaty article.

c) They concluded that any organ of state could be liable under the principle.

d) They concluded that the Member State must have manifestly and gravely disregard the limits on its discretion.

Free Movement of Goods

1) Of the cases listed below, which one lays down the conditions for the payment of a legitimate fee for a service when entering a member state?

a) Commission v Belgium (Customs Warehouses)

b) Commission v Italy (Art Treasures)

c) Commission v Germany (Animal Inspections)

d) Commission v Italy (Statistical Levy)

2) Of the following, which is NOT a requirement according to Commission v Germany (Animal Inspections) as regards inspections necessary in EU law?

a) The charge must not exceed the cost of the inspections.

b) The inspections must be prescribed by EU law.

c) The inspections must be of benefit to the importer.

d) The inspections must promote the free movement of goods.

3) Which one of the following is NOT a condition for the payment of a valid fee?

a) The goods must be similar.

b) It is consideration for a payment rendered.

c) It is of benefit to the importer.

d) The amount charged is commensurate with the costs of the service provided.

4) Which of the cases listed below constitutes the basis of the idea that the existence of grounds for charging a fee does NOT imply that the fee is lawful?

a) Diamanterbeiders

b) Commission v Italy (Art Treasures)

c) van Gend en Loos

d) Commission v the Netherlands

5) Which one is NOT the defense mechanism under Article 36?

a) Public policy

b) Public security

c) Protection of industrial and commercial property

d) National security

6) Who is NOT bound by Article 34?

a) Royal Pharmaceutical Society

b) The Law Society

c) Tesco

d) Local Authorities

7) Which one of the following situations is NOT as an example of a charge which will not fall within Article 30?

a) Interest of the importer

b) Payment for a service rendered

c) Inspections required by EU law or international treaties

d) Internal dues

8) Which one of the following does NOT engage with internal taxation?

a) Humblot

b) Reprographic Machinery

c) Regenerated Oil

d) Commission v Germany (Animal Inspections)

9) Which one of the following does NOT engage with Article 110(2) - non-similar products?

a) Commission v France (Sprits)

b) Commission v UK (Wine and Beer)

c) Commission v Belgium

d) Commission v Germany (Animal Inspections)

10) Which of the following contains the key definition of a QR?

a) R v Henn and Darby

b) International Fruit Co (No 2)

c) Geddo v Ente Nazionale Risi

d) Firma Denkavit Futtermittel GMBH

11) Which of the following contains the definition of an MEQR?

   a)   Dassonville

   b)   International Fruit Co (No 2)

   c)   Geddo v Ente Nazionale Risi

   d)   Firma Denkavit Futtermittel GMBH

12) Which of the following cases concerns a distinctly applicable MEQR?

   a)   Walter Rau

   b)   Verein v Mars

   c)   Commission v Denmark (Danish Beer Cans)

   d)   Commission v Ireland (Irish Souvenirs)

13) Which case concerns an indistinctly applicable MEQR?

   a)   Buy Irish

   b)   Cinetheque

   c)   Irish Souvenirs

   d)   Conegate

14) Which case introduced the concept of a selling arrangement?

   a)   Torfaen BC v B&Q

   b)   Keck & Mithouard

   c)   Cassis de Dijon

   d)   Stoke-on –Trent v B&Q

15) In Cassis de Dijon, which rule is relied upon by the importers?

   a)   Rule of reason

   b)   Payment for benefit

   c)   Presumption of mutual recognition

   d)   Equal in law and in fact

Free Movement of Person

1) Directive 2004/38 grants the right to move freely within the territory of the European Union to…

- a) Students
- b) Workers
- c) Citizens
- d) All of the above

2) Which three of the following criteria are parts of the Lawrie-Blum 'worker' test (More than one option may be selected):

- a) Person must perform service
- b) Person must perform public service
- c) For and under the direction of another person
- d) in one of the Member States
- e) in return for money
- f) in return for remuneration
- g) and contribute towards household costs

3) Individuals in part-time employment can satisfy the EU 'worker' test.

- a) True
- b) False

4) For how long may individuals seeking employment remain on the territory of a host Member State?

- a) For up to 36 months.
- b) For up to 12 months.
- c) For up to 6 months.
- d) For as long as necessary to find employment provided, they are 'genuinely seeking employment for a reasonable time'.

5) Which of these cases concerns job-seekers?

a) Cowan

b) Lair

c) Antonissen

d) Steymann

6) Which one of the following a worker would NOT be able to bring to the host Member State with them?

a) Their children

b) Their parents

c) Their dependants

d) Descendants of Partners

e) Non-EU spouses

f) Non-EU ex-spouse not holding custody of the child

7) Will divorce affect non-economically active person's right to reside in the host Member State?

a) Yes, if they are a third country national

b) No, if they are an EU citizen

c) No, if they hold custody of a child

d) No, if they were married less than 3 years

8) For how long can an EU citizen enter and reside in another member State without any additional formalities?

a) Three months

b) Two months

c) Three weeks

d) Ninety days

9) For how long should an EU citizen have lived on the territory of the host state to acquire the permanent right to reside there?

a) Three years

b) Five years

c) Ten years

d) Seven years

10) What is the fundamental prerequisite for EU citizens as regards their being legally within the borders of another Member State?

a) They should not be economically active.

b) They should not become a burden on the social welfare system of the host state.

c) They should claim state-sponsored medical treatments.

d) They should not claim any financial benefits.

11) Workers have which of the rights listed below? (More than one option may be selected)

a) right to social and economic benefits

b) right to education

c) exemption from taxes in the Member State other than their country of origin

d) freedom from discrimination

12) Which of the following could be used as grounds for expulsion for EU workers?

a) Past criminal convictions alone

b) Evidence that a person presents a threat to the public

c) Contagious flu condition

d) EU worker is qualified in an oversubscribed area of employment

13) For a person to be deported from a host Member State on the grounds of public policy which of the following must be demonstrated? (More than one option may be selected)

a) The existence of an ongoing threat to the public

b) On entering the Member state, the individual must arouse the suspicion of the customs officer

c) The individual needs to pose a reasonably serious threat

d) All the above options

14) Article 7(2) of Regulation 492/2011 stipulates that an employee who is a citizen of Member State 'shall enjoy the same social and tax advantages as national workers'.

a) True

b) False

15) Which one is NOT the derogation ground under Article 45(3)?

a) Public policy

b) Public security

c) Public health

d) Economic well-being of the country

Establishment and Services

1) Which article contains the right to freedom of establishment?

a) Article 48

b) Article 49

c) Article 55

d) Article 56

2) Of the following, who possesses the right to freedom of establishment?

a) Professional people or those involved in trade

b) Self-employed individuals

c) Professional individuals or those involved in trade and self-employed persons

d) Undertakings, agencies, branches, subsidiaries, self-employed persons

3) Which of the following statements are correct? (More than one option may be selected)

a) Nondiscrimination based on nationality is only applicable to Freedom of Establishment.

b) Nondiscrimination based on nationality relates to both Freedom of Establishment and the Freedom to Provide Services.

c) There is no restriction anticipated to the duration of both the Freedom of Establishment and the Freedom to Provide Services.

d) While there is no restriction anticipated to the duration of the Freedom of Establishment, the Freedom to Provide Services is more short-term.

4) When reaching a decision on whether an activity is temporary or permanent, which of the following issues does the court consider?

a) Duration

b) Periodicity

c) Regularity

d) Continuity

e) All of the above

5) Of the following points, which are applicable in the event of there being no EU rules standardising entry qualifications for a profession? (More than one option may be selected)

a) Every Member State has the right to implement rules on admittance to professions in its territory.

b) Every Member State has the right to implement rules on admittance to professions in its territory as long as these rules are not discriminate as regards nationality.

c) The acceptable standard of qualifications shall be guaranteed by means of reciprocal recognition of the equivalence of qualifications, to be judged objectively.

d) Authorities in a Member state have an obligation to evaluate an applicant's education, training, knowledge and acquired skills and to make a comparison with what is required in that state.

6) Which of the following statement is correct in the context of freedom of establishment? (More than one option may be selected)

a) It only applies to purely internal situations.

b) It only applies to purely external situations.

c) It only applies internally in cases where there is a European Union or cross border element.

d) It only applies externally in cases where there is a European Union or cross border element.

7) Which of the following statements is correct? (More than one option may be selected)

a) Member States have an obligation to comply with any directive that establishes professional standards and may disregard their own national standards.

b) Member States have an obligation to comply with any directive establishing professional standards and disregard their own national standards.

c) In the absence of a directive case law must be complied with and Member States may consider the qualifications and experience of an individual.

d) In the absence of a directive case law must be complied with and Member States must consider the qualifications and experience of an individual.

8) Which Article includes derogation grounds from the freedom of establishment? (More than one option may be selected)

a) 49

b) 50

c) 51

d) 52

9) Which of the following allow derogation from the freedom of establishment?

a) The exercise of official authority

b) On the grounds of public policy, public health or public security

c) All of the above

d) None of the above

10) Which Article does the right of freedom to provide services contain?

a)   Article 48

b)   Article 49

c)   Article 55

d)   Article 56

11) To whom does the right of freedom to provide services apply? (More than one option may be selected)

a)   Individuals and companies providing services within their own Member State

b)   Individuals who travel to other Member States to receive services

c)   Individuals who have moved to another Member State temporarily to provide a service

d)   Companies based in one Member State who are providing services to someone in another Member State

12) Which of the following statements are correct?

a)   The Freedom to Provide Services does not have direct effect.

b)   The Freedom to Provide Services has vertical direct effect.

c)   The Freedom to Provide Services has horizontal direct effect.

d)   The Freedom to Provide Services has vertical and horizontal direct effect.

13) A company can be established in a Member State even if it does not carry out any trading there:

a)   True

b)   False

14) What rights are granted by the freedom to provide services?

a)   The right to move in another Member State to provide services

b)   The right to reside in another Member State to provide services

c)   The right to operate as a business in another Member State

d)   All of the above

15) The right to freedom to provide services applies to:

    a) Measures which directly discriminate against service providers

    b) Measures which indirectly discriminate against service providers

    c) Both of the above

    d) None of the above

Competition Law

1) In which one of the following cases did the Commission give a clear definition of a concerted practice?

    a) ICI v Commission (Dyestuffs)

    b) A.B.G. Oil

    c) Knoors

    d) Levin

2) Of the articles listed below, in which are 'hardcore items' covered by Art 101 to be found?

    a) Article 101(1)

    b) Article 101(2)

    c) Article 101(3)

    d) Article 101(4)

3) Which one of the following was the defence of de minimis established at below 10% for horizontal agreements?

    a) Commission Notice

    b) UK Act of Parliament

    c) Volk v Vervaecke

    d) UK Statutory Instrument

4) In order to meet the conditions for a block exemption as enshrined in Article 101(3), which of the characteristics below must an agreement possess?

    a)   Allow consumers a fair share of any benefit

    b)   Have neither dispensable restrictions nor significantly undermine competition in the market in question

    c)   Enhance the production or distribution of goods and encourage technical or economic advancement

    d)   All of the above

5) What type of agreement does the case of United Brands provide an example of?

    a)   Gentleman's agreement

    b)   Oral agreement

    c)   Vertical agreement

    d)   Horizontal agreement

6) In which one of the following cases was 'dominance' established as being 'a position of economic strength enjoyed by an undertaking which enables it to behave...to an appreciable extent independently of its competitors, customers and ultimately of its consumers'?

    a)   Akzo Chemie BV v Commission

    b)   Hilti AG v Commission

    c)   United Brands Co v Commission

    d)   Tetrapak Rausing SA v Commission

7) Which one of the following will NOT fall within the scope of Article 101?

    a)   The unilateral adoption of a policy by one undertaking in the context of its continuing business.

    b)   Co-ordination between undertakings which knowingly substitutes practical cooperation between them for the risks of competition.

    c)   An informal gentleman's agreement between undertakings.

    d)   A recommendation by a trade association to its members.

8) The judgment of the Court of Justice in United Brands is a landmark decision for several principles regarding Article 102. Of the following principles which one is NOT covered by this judgment?

a) That large scale undercutting of prices may constitute the abuse of a dominant position.

b) That a dominant position signifies the economic power of an undertaking.

c) That the extent of vertical integration may be relevant in defining dominance.

d) That the clearly defined geographic market is the sphere in which the circumstances of competition attached to the product are alike for all undertakings.

9) What is meant by a vertical agreement?

a) An agreement between an undertaking and the State.

b) An agreement which creates a hierarchy between undertakings.

c) An agreement between undertakings at different levels of trade or industry.

d) An agreement involving a chain of relationships between several undertakings.

10) Which option is NOT the relevant market?

a) The Relevant Product Market

b) The Relevant Geographic Market

c) The Relevant Temporal Market

d) Market Share

11) Which one is NOT the factors of establishing dominance?

a) Market Share

b) Intellectual Property

c) Vertical Integration

d) Relevant Geographic Market

12) Which one is NOT the abusive behaviour?

a) Refusal to supply

b) Predatory pricing

c) Excessive prices

d) Reasonable discounts

13) Article 101(3) sets out two positive and two negative conditions

a) True

b) False

14) Having a dominant position in a market constitutes, by itself, a breach of Article 102.

a) True

b) False

15) Which of the following regulations are related to block exemptions? (More than one option may be selected)

a) Regulation 330/2010

b) Regulation 1/2003

c) Regulation 492/2011

d) Regulation 305/2011

ANSWERS

Direct Applicability/Direct Effect/Indirect Effect/State Liability

1) d; 2) a and b; 3) a; 4) a; 5) c; 6) b and d; 7) b; 8) d; 9) b; 10) a; 11) c; 12) a; 13) b; 14) c; 15) a, c and d

Free Movement of Goods

1) a; 2) c; 3) a; 4) b; 5) d; 6) c; 7) a; 8) d; 9) d; 10) c; 11) a; 12) d; 13) b; 14) b; 15) c

Free Movement of Person

1) d; 2) a, c and f; 3) a; 4) d; 5) c; 6) f; 7) c; 8) a; 9) b; 10) b; 11) a, b and d; 12) b; 13) a and c; 14) a; 15) d

Establishment and Services

1) b; 2) d; 3) b and d; 4) e; 5) b, c and d; 6) c and d; 7) b and d; 8) c and d; 9) c; 10) d; 11) b, c and d; 12) d; 13) a; 14) d; 15) c

Competition Law

1) a; 2) a; 3) a; 4) d; 5) c; 6) c; 7) a; 8) a; 9) c; 10) d; 11) d; 12) d; 13) a; 14) b; 15) a and b

RECOMMENDED READING LIST

Barents, R., 'Charges of Equivalent Effect to Customs Duties', (1978), 15 CMLRev 415.

Barnard, C., *The Substantive Law of the EU*, 6th edition, Oxford University Press, 2019.

Chalmers, D., Davies, G. and Monti, G., *European Union Law: Text and Materials*, 4th edition, Cambridge University Press, 2019.

Dinan, P. D., Europe Recast: A History of European Union, Palgrave, 2004.

Drake, S., '20 years After Von Colson: the Impact of 'Indirect Effect' on the Protection of the Individuals Community Rights', (2005), 30 ELR 329.

Ewan, K, *Law Express: EU Law*, Pearson, 2008.

Fairhurst, J., *Law of the European Union*, 10th edition, Pearson, 2014.

Golynker, O., 'Jobseekers' Rights in the European Union: Challenges of Changing the Paradigm of Social Solidarity', (2005), ELRev 111.

Homewood, M., *Concentrate EU Law*, Oxford University Press, 2016.

Horspool, M. and Humphreys, M., *European Union Law*, 10th edition, Oxford University Press, 2018.

Nassimdian, D., 'And We Keep on Meeting: (De)fragmenting State Liability', (2007), 32 ELR 819.

Oppenheimer, A., 'The Relantionship between European Community Law and National Law, Cambridge University Press, 2004.

Prechal, S., *Directives in EC Law*, Oxford University Press, 2006.

Robertson, B., 'What Is a Restriction of Competition? The Implications of the CFIs Judgment in O2 Germany and the Rule of Reason', (2007), ECLR 59.

Schrauwen, A. and Prinssen, J., *Direct Effect: Rethinking a Classic of EC Legal Doctrine*, Europa Law Publishing, 2004.

Schütze, R., *European Union Law*, 2nd edition, Cambridge University Press, 2018.

Sharp, K. and Pommel, C., *The Law of the European Union*, BPP Law School: London, 2018.

Shuibhne, N., 'The Free Movement of Goods and Article 28: An Evolving Framework', (2002), 27 ELR 408.

Siemms, M., 'Convergance, Competition, Centros and Conflicts of Law', (2002), 27 ELR 47.

Urwin, D., The Community of Europe: A History of European Integration Since 1945, Longman, 1994.

Van Gerven, G. and Varona, E., 'The Wood Pulp Case and the Future of Concerted Practices', (1994), 31 CMLRev 575.

Woods, L., Watson, P. and Costa, M., *Steiner and Woods EU Law*, 13th edition, Oxford University Press, 2017.

INDEX

115

Printed in Great Britain
by Amazon